40 DAYS TO A FORTIFIED LIFE

"Forty Biblical References, Forty Fundamental Insights, Forty Days of Fulfillment"

HILETTE A. VIRGO

40 Days to a Fortified Life

Published by

Great-Nest Publishing Inc.

Cover Design: Calbert Simpson

Acknowledgment

I Am So Happy to Be His Pen

I am so happy to be His pen,
A vessel of words, not of men.
Ink flows freely, guided true,
By the hand that makes all things new.

No burden weighs upon my soul,
For He who writes has full control.
Each stroke of grace, each line of light,
Shines with great truth both bold and bright.

I do not strive to make my mark,
Nor fear my voice fades in the dark.
For if He wills, the world will read,
And find in words the strength they need.

I am so happy to be His pen,
To speak His love again and again.
Not for fame nor fleeting praise,
But to echo heaven's glorious rays.

So let Him write, let Him lead,
Through willing hands that plant His seed.
For *40 Days to a Fortified Life* I stand,
A pen of purpose in His hand.

But even the strongest pen needs a steady hand,

And every calling requires a faithful band.

For though He speaks and guides my way,

He places souls to light my stay.

In this season, I have been blessed with four earthly pillars of inspiration who have stood beside me, anchoring me with love, wisdom, and support to complete this work.

Special thanks to Cheryl Butts and Serena Rowe, my prayer warrior, sounding board sisters, and Bible study partners. Your faith and intercession have covered my life, reinforcing my spirit when the weight of the journey felt heavy. To Samantha Campbell, my unpaid therapist and encourager, your words have been a balm, soothing the weary moments and reminding me to press forward. And last but certainly not least, my Queen Sonia Virgo, the matriarch of my heart, who birthed and groomed me to birth books, whose grace, strength, and presence continue to inspire me to walk in purpose.

Finally, a heartfelt thank you to my team at Great-Nest Publishing Inc. and Melcardo Blackwood for tangibly supporting this project. Your generosity and belief in this vision have made an impact beyond words.

Hilette Virgo

TABLE OF CONTENTS

PREFACE

For years, the number 40 beckoned to me. Every time I encountered it in Scripture, something sparked within me. I remember a conversation with a friend who was approaching this sacred milestone. I confidently told him that 40 represented a significant shift and that he would experience a new walk. I envision him entering his 40th year as passing through the Red Sea or the Jordan River, undergoing a purge, a transformation, and a maturity process. I just felt deep in my spirit that 40 meant something far more profound than what met the eye.

Years earlier, my dear friend Nadian Reid was approaching this milestone, and we found ourselves marveling at the biblical significance of 40. Our discussion was more than an intellectual exercise; it was a divine moment of revelation. She shared how God had revealed to her that her trials leading up to this age mirrored the Israelites' wanderings, a prelude to deliverance. She spoke of an impending turnaround and the fulfillment of His promises. It was a prophetic utterance, and I had the privilege of witnessing His transformative power unfold in her life—breakthroughs from childhood trauma and newfound freedom in various aspects of her journey. Looking back, I see that moment not as happenstance but as divine foreshadowing. Some might call it fate; I call it a seed planted for an obsession that would fully bloom half a decade later. (Nadian, if you're reading this—consider yourself my co-conspirator in this numerical adventure!)

Little did I know that my curiosity would be fully awakened when a passage of Scripture reignited the intrigue.

This time, I couldn't resist the pull. I found myself staying up into the early hours, scouring the Word, the internet, and Bible scholarly writings to uncover every significant mention of the number 40. What began as curiosity soon became an avalanche of discovery. I started numbering each reference in my flowery preaching journal, an impression I now recognize as the Holy Spirit's leading.

When I reached the thirties, I felt an urgent desire to keep searching until I reached 40. Wouldn't it be incredible if there were precisely 40 significant mentions of 40 in the Bible? By the time I reached 34, I was exhausted but still yearning for more. Lord, there has to be more. Stimulation gave way to sheer exhaustion, and I surrendered to sleep. The next morning, I woke up with renewed energy and excitement, but after a few days, I moved on from the subject.

Three months later, the instructions came with undeniable clarity:

"Put the information you gleaned in a book."

As I wrote, fresh insights poured in, and God revealed things beyond my research. This was confirmation that this is a God-ordained, approved work because He didn't stop pouring until I reached 40. In fact, after completing the manuscript, He instructed me to restructure it—placing what was originally the last chapter as the first and concluding the book with Jesus's ascension and an invitation to prepare for our heavenly flight. I take no credit for the order and flow; I was merely an instrument in this work.

Having published hundreds of books and authored six of my own prior, writing a book is as natural to me as taking a shower. So, I instinctively began exploring titles. Within minutes, the title came, and the book began to take shape. But this was no ordinary book—it was God's gift to me for my personal transformation.

For years, the Lord had been calling me to step into His presence for an intimate 40-day expedition—just as Elijah, Moses, and Jesus had. Not necessarily with a physical fast, or in the manner that many Christians celebrate Lent annually, but with a heart and mind fully surrendered to intentional communion with Him. This book became my pathway to that journey. And if just one person decides to join me on this pilgrimage, that would be a bonus.

A forty-day journey is a phenomenon that Christians have embraced for centuries. Lent, a period of fasting, prayer, and reflection leading up to Easter, is one of the most well-known examples of a forty-day spiritual practice. Its origins date back to the 4th century, modeled after Jesus' own forty days of fasting in the wilderness. Many believers embark on a forty-day journey during this season, dedicating themselves to repentance, spiritual renewal, and preparation for the celebration of Christ's resurrection.

However, a forty-day journey is not confined to Lent—it can be taken at any time. This book is not just an invitation to follow a ritual but an opportunity to make your forty days deeply personal and as unique as your relationship with God. Whether you are using this book during the Lenten season or at another significant point in your life, this journey is about transformation, fortification, and deepening your connection with the Lord.

This book is the first installment in the series, *Sacred Numbers: Unlocking God's Divine Code in Scripture.* It is a foundational exploration into the profound symbolism of 40, setting the stage for deeper dives into other numbers that carry divine significance.

How to Use This Book

Since you've chosen to take this journey, allow me to offer a few pointers.

You may choose to read the devotionals each morning, using the reflections to shape your daily prayers. Let these 40 biblical references to the number 40 enrich your walk with Christ.

You can also use this as an opportunity to fast—whether through the Daniel fast (consuming only fruits and water) or by tailoring your own version of fasting. Perhaps you'll choose to fast from social media, movies, entertainment, certain foods, or other distractions. Structure it in a way that suits your lifestyle and spiritual goals.

This is 40 days of connecting the Bible's references to 40—from creation to Christ's ascension. The Bible does not explicitly mention the 40-week gestation process, yet this is one of the most beautiful displays of God's creative power. That theme, the divine process of formation and transformation—is subtly woven throughout this devotional, like a fragrance carried on the winds of application.

A Journey to Transformation

While writing this book, I shared my discoveries with several friends, and their excitement fueled my own. Brother Gerald

Gray and Dr. A. Dodridge Bowers were especially enthusiastic about seeing the finished work, adding extra zeal to my completion of it.

As a Christian Life Coach, I am inspired to use this book as a tool for intentional spiritual transformation. That's why I created the *40 Days to a Fortified Life Coaching Guide* and *The Fortification Journal*—two powerful resources to maximize your experience.

- The Coaching Guide contains activities and coaching insights designed to help you go deeper in your journey.
- The Fortification Journal will be your personal space to reflect, record, and document your transformation.

If you desire this enhanced experience, I encourage you to get both resources. If you prefer a one-on-one coaching experience, feel free to contact me at:

hilettevirgomotivates@gmail.com
greatnestpublications@gmail.com

You, too, will be thrilled to meet the new version of yourself at the end of these 40 days. Brace yourself for the glow, the shift, and the renewed mindset. Prepare to fall deeper in love with God and ignite a desire to know Him more intimately.

- If you are yet to approach 40, this book is perfect for you.
- If you are in your forties, it is ideal.
- If you are beyond your forties, it is a necessary read.

Gift or recommend this book to someone 40 days before their birthday milestone, anniversary, or a major life event. This book is an invitation to enter a new level with God and to join the ranks of the patriarchs, prophets, judges, kings, and apostles who experienced the number forty celestially.

I look forward to hearing the testimonies of your transformation.

With faith and fortitude,

Hilette Virgo

INTRODUCTION

For years, every time I set sail on the boundless, unpredictable seas of spiritual exploration, the number 40 would appear on the horizon—sometimes as a gentle whisper, like a breeze rustling through the pages of an old book, and other times as a neon sign flashing and bobbing on the tides in bold capped prints, "PAY ATTENTION!" It drifted toward me in waves, tugging at my curiosity, beckoning me to follow.

So, like any good explorer, I did. I dropped my anchor, docked my ship, and waded through the shallows of the bay as I approached the shore. I gathered the forties scattered like manna on the shoreline—easy to spot, ready to be picked up and savored. But others were hidden, tucked away like buried treasure, requiring me to dig deep, searching the scriptures like a miner hunting for gold. I followed the divine sparks, until I stumbled upon something unexpected—a narrow opening in the great Tree of Revelation.

Of course, being the adventurous type (or just too intrigued to turn back), I stepped inside. That's when I realized that this wasn't some peaceful stroll along the coastline. Oh no, I had just buckled myself into a spiritual rollercoaster, and God Himself was the ride operator. The kind who doesn't give you a heads-up before the first drop.

And so, I held on for dear life as I plummeted through the Scriptures, discovering a breathtaking pattern. Forty days. Forty years. Again, and again. Sparkling and beckoning, waiting to be uncovered. Forty days of rain to reset the world. Forty days of revelation on Mount Sinai. Forty years of wandering that felt like an eternal road trip without GPS. Every time the number appeared, something shifted—something was fortified.

God, the Master of mysteries and divine intrigue, has always worked in layers. His wisdom is carved into the sacred design of creation itself, and the number 40 is one of His most intriguing imprints. Think about it—when He made the first human, He sculpted him with His own hands, carefully forming a full-grown man from the dust of the earth, then He sculpted a woman from his rib. But when it came to the rest of us, God put a different plan into motion. He designed an intricate 40-week process of gestation, where a delicate, unseen miracle unfolds in secret before a tiny, precious life is expelled into the world. And from that first breath, we begin to cycle through forties.

Forty days of testing. Forty days of transformation. Forty years of growing, wandering, learning. Again and again, God uses this number to mark seasons of trial and triumph, waiting and revelation, breaking and rebuilding.

This book is a devotional journey through these forty follicles—divine moments rooted in Scripture, each carrying a lesson waiting to be unearthed. Every day, we will explore one of these biblical forties, breaking open its meaning like fresh manna from heaven. And because wisdom is best absorbed through action, each devotional ends with a reflection and affirmation to fortify the message—because truth isn't just meant to be read; it's meant to be lived.

Treasure hunting isn't just for kids. Whether you're young or old, there's something thrilling about seeking, finding, and unlocking mysteries. That's exactly what this book invites you to do. To go on a sacred treasure hunt through the Word of God, discovering the forties He has hidden like clues in a grand adventure.

So, gather your family, grab your spiritual map, sign the commitment statement as a promise to yourself, and let's embark on this journey together. This is 40 Days to a Fortified Life—and trust me, the treasure waiting at the end is worth it.

40-Day Commitment Statement

I, _______________, commit to embarking on this 40-day journey to a fortified life. I acknowledge that this is not just a reading plan, but a transformative experience that requires my full dedication—spiritually, mentally, and emotionally. Over the next forty days, I will engage with the devotionals, reflect on their lessons, and apply them to my daily life.

I commit to seeking God's presence, deepening my faith, and allowing His Word to shape me. I will remain consistent, intentional, and open to His divine revelations. I understand that fortification is a process, and I am willing to endure the refining, stretching, and strengthening that comes with it.

By signing this, I declare that I am ready to be transformed, empowered, and fortified for the journey ahead.

Signature: ____________________________

Date: ________________________________

DAY 1

FORTY WEEKS OF FORMATION: THE DIVINE BLUEPRINT OF LIFE

Welcome to Day 1 of the Fortified Life! Today, you stand at the threshold of something extraordinary—a journey of formation, growth, and transformation. This is not just a study, or another devotional. Think of it as a divine boot camp, where God Himself is your trainer, sculpting and strengthening you for the journey ahead. Unlike a traditional workout, there are no dumbbells involved—just the weight of His wisdom pressing into every fiber of your being. Over the next days, as you weave through the 40 meandering messages, you will emerge fortified and faith-filled.

Though the number 40 is not explicitly mentioned in the creation story, its imprint is there in a subtle but significant way. From the moment the first human was formed, God set in motion the blueprint of life itself—a process that mirrors the very way we enter the world.

> *"Then the Lord God formed the man from the dust of the ground. He breathed the breath of life into the man's nostrils, and the man became a living person."*
> ***(Genesis 2:7)***

Just as Adam was shaped by the hands of God, so were you—both physically and spiritually. Before you took your first breath, God was already at work, forming your bones, your purpose, and your destiny. The forty-week gestation period in the womb is no accident. It is a divine pattern—a period crucial for a child's proper development, growth, and survival. Likewise, this forty-day journey will see you being shaped, strengthened, and spiritually developed to step into your purpose. (And thankfully, this one doesn't require an umbilical cord!)

This concept of divine formation continues in the story of the first human birth recorded in Scripture—Cain. He was the firstborn of humanity, the tangible result of God's creation mandate to "be fruitful and multiply." His birth was evidence of the continuation of God's divine design.

> *"Now Adam knew Eve his wife, and she conceived and bore Cain, saying, 'I have gotten a man with the help of the Lord.'"*
> ***(Genesis 4:1)***

From the first birth to every life thereafter, including yours, God has been intricately involved in the formation process. The 40-week cycle of gestation is not directly referenced in the Bible, but it is an established biological fact supported by medical science, embryology, and obstetrics. This cycle testifies to the mysterious and marvelous character of God, who designs, develops, and brings forth life according to His perfect timing.

> *"Your eyes saw my unformed body; all the days ordained for me were written in Your book before one of them came to be."*
> ***(Psalm 139:16)***

Before you had form, before your heart took its first beat, God saw you. He devised your development in the womb, ensuring that each stage prepared you for life outside of it. In the same way a fetus develops vital organs, bones, and muscles to survive outside the womb, this journey will equip you with the spiritual muscles, endurance, and faith necessary to thrive in God's calling.

As you delve deeper into this book or study the Bible, you will notice that God has instances when He declares a day-for-a-year model. For this devotional, we will apply a day-for-a-week in the gestation process of your fortification through cycles of forty. Over the next forty days, you will uncover marvelous references to the number 40 throughout the Bible, each one revealing God's process of preparation, testing, and transformation. This is your preparation phase—your spiritual gestation. What is forming in you during this time will determine how you step into the next season of your life.

Reflection:

- What areas of my life need spiritual formation and strengthening?
- Am I willing to surrender to God's process, even when I don't fully understand it?
- What am I expecting to be "birthed" in my life by the end of this journey?

Affirmation:

I am divinely formed and fashioned by the hands of my Creator. Every moment of my life has been orchestrated by His perfect wisdom. I embrace this journey of transformation with faith, knowing that God is preparing me for something greater. I am being fortified, strengthened, and made ready for my destiny. I am not just existing—I am being shaped for purpose.

DAY 2

A Cleansing Flood

Welcome to Day 2! You have been fertilized, implanted, and properly initiated for this journey of growth. After God created the world perfectly, mankind's character was marred by sin. The once pure and untainted creation was now corrupted, leading to separation from the Creator. But in His mercy, God devised a plan—not of destruction, but of renewal. Humanity needed a second chance, a fresh start, and a cleansing process to begin again.

God desires to fortify your life—purging the old, refining your heart, and equipping you for the path ahead. Today marks the second day of that process, a fresh start just as the flood was for the world.

> *"And the rain was upon the earth forty days and forty nights."*
> ***(Genesis 7:12)***

From creation to the flood, approximately 1,656 years had passed, according to biblical genealogies recorded in Genesis 5. Over this timeframe, the harmonious relationship between God and humanity had eroded. Humanity had turned its back on God, embracing corruption and defying His ways. Despite 120 years of warnings, the people refused to repent. Finally, judgment came in the form of a cleansing flood. For forty days and nights, relentless rain poured down, purging the land, washing away wickedness, and resetting the atmosphere. This was not just destruction—it was divine purification. God wanted to cleanse, purge, and renew the earth, offering humanity a new beginning.

God's renewal plan wasn't for everyone—it was for eight people. Why eight? In biblical numerology, eight represents new beginnings. As a factor of forty, it fits perfectly into God's restoration plan. Through Noah and his family, the world would start over, demonstrating God's grace and the power of a fresh start. Just as Noah's ark carried them safely through the storm, God is preparing you for transformation, carrying you through your own spiritual renewal.

The flood is the Bible's first reference to the number forty, a symbol of transformation and preparation. In the same way, God desires to wash away everything in your life that keeps you from Him. Just as the waters purified the earth, He longs to cleanse your heart, removing sin, doubt, and burdens. As Ezekiel 36:25 (KJV) declares, "Then will I sprinkle clean water upon you, and ye shall be clean: from all your filthiness, and from all your idols, will I cleanse you." This process can feel overwhelming—like being caught in a downpour—but God's purpose is not to destroy you; it is to restore you. He wants to make you whole.

God wants to save, cleanse, and purge you. The flood didn't just remove evil—it created a new opportunity. See this devotional as your own fresh start. God is washing away the past so that you can step forward in faith, unburdened and renewed. Trust His process, surrender to His cleansing, and embrace the transformation He has in store for you.

Reflection:

- What areas in your life need cleansing?
- Are there sins, habits, or mindsets God is calling you to release?
- Have you ever felt spiritually weighed down? How can you invite God's cleansing today?
- How does knowing that God's cleansing is meant to restore rather than destroy change your perspective?
- What steps can you take to embrace this fresh start?

Affirmation:

I embrace God's cleansing in my life. I release every burden, every sin, and every mindset that holds me back. Like Noah, I step into the ark of God's protection, trusting that He is preparing me for something greater. I am renewed, restored, and fortified. I walk forward in faith, knowing that my fresh start is divinely orchestrated.

DAY 3

THE ARK OF TRUST

Welcome to Day 3! At this point in your journey, you are an embryo, and something remarkable is happening—your neural tube is beginning to develop. In biological terms, this structure is the foundation for your brain and spinal cord, the very system that will allow you to function, think, and move. But spiritually? Your neural tube represents something even greater—the framework of trust in God that will guide you through life's uncertainties. Just as your body is being formed with precision, so too is your faith being structured, strengthened, and secured for the days ahead.

Yesterday, we focused on God's cleansing power, how He washes away what is impure to make way for something new. Today, we shift our focus to trust—learning to rest in God's protection, just as Noah did when the floodwaters lifted the ark.

> *"And the flood was forty days upon the earth; and the waters increased, and bare up the ark, and it was lift up above the earth."*
> ***— Genesis 7:17 (KJV)***

Notice that the ark wasn't just floating aimlessly—it was lifted for forty days. The waters didn't just bring destruction; they elevated Noah and his family, separating them from the corruption of the world. What seemed like a catastrophe was actually a divine elevation. The same waters that overwhelmed the earth became the vehicle of God's preservation for those who trusted Him.

Life's trials can feel like raging floods, threatening to pull us under. Fear, uncertainty, and hardship may rise around us, but if we are in the ark of God's presence, we will not be lost. Instead, God uses what seems overwhelming to lift us closer to Him. Your trust is your ark. Just as Noah followed God's design precisely, we, too, must build our lives according to His Word, trusting that when the storms come, He will bear us up.

For forty days, the ark remained above the earth. Forty days—set apart, sustained, and secured by God's hand. This wasn't an accident; it was a divine blueprint, a clear pattern of preservation through obedience. In this forty-day journey of spiritual formation, you are not just floating through random devotionals—you are being fortified in faith. God is lifting you higher, shaping your trust, and preparing you for what is to come.

Reflection:

- What situations in your life feel overwhelming, like floodwaters rising around you?
- How has God used past difficulties to strengthen your faith?
- In what ways can you trust Him to bear you up today?

Affirmation:

I am safe in the ark of God's presence. No storm, no flood, and no uncertainty can separate me from His protection. I choose to trust in His plan, knowing that He is using every challenge to elevate me. I am set apart, sustained, and secured by His mighty hand. My trust is my ark, and in Him, I will rise above the storm.

DAY 4

THE WINDOW OF HOPE

Welcome to Day 4! Something miraculous has happened—your heart is now beating. Just as an embryo's heart begins to pulse around the fourth week, signaling the emergence of life, today marks a spiritual quickening in your journey. The cleansing waters have done their work, and the ark has been lifted. Now, it's time to open your window of hope.

Noah endured forty days of relentless rain, a period of judgment and transformation, but his waiting wasn't over. He remained in the ark, enclosed in God's protection, until another forty-day period had passed. And then, something changed—Noah opened the window.

> *"And it came to pass at the end of forty days, that Noah opened the window of the ark which he had made."*
> ***— Genesis 8:6 (KJV)***

This was more than just a physical act—it was an act of faith. He had no guarantee of what lay beyond the wooden walls of his waiting season, yet he opened the window, expecting to see the evidence of God's next move.

Just as an embryo's first heartbeat confirms life's momentum, Noah's act of opening the window signified spiritual movement—a shift from passive endurance to active expectation. It was the first step toward stepping into the new world God was preparing. Similarly, in your journey, God is calling you to move from waiting to watching—to open a window of faith and seek signs of what He is unfolding beyond your current circumstances.

Noah's patience had been tested, but forty days later, his waiting took on new meaning. The storm had passed, but the earth was still covered in water. The transition was not yet complete. And yet, he took a step forward—he made a small move of trust, rather than rushing ahead.

Are you in a season where the rain has stopped, but you're still surrounded by uncertainty? God invites you to open your own window of faith, to look beyond the ark of protection and glimpse the hope that is rising. Though you may not see dry land yet, trust that God is working beneath the surface to bring you into a new season.

Reflection:

- Are you in a season of waiting where God is asking you to open a window of faith?
- In what areas of your life do you need to lift your eyes from your circumstances and trust in what God is preparing ahead?
- How does recognizing the significance of another forty-day period deepen your understanding of God's process in your life?

Just as Noah didn't stay in the ark forever, your season of waiting is not permanent. This was the second cycle of forty, a sign that God was once again guiding a transformation. When the time is right, God will show you the next step. Keep your window open for His direction.

Affirmation:

I choose to open the window of faith in my life. I trust that God is working behind the scenes, preparing the next step in my journey. Though I may not see the full picture yet, I believe that His plans for me are unfolding perfectly. My hope is in Him, and I am expectant for the new season He is bringing into my life.

DAY 5

PARTNERING WITH GOD FOR DIVINE PURPOSE

Welcome to Day 5! As we continue our journey of fortification, we transition from the waiting and watching of Noah to the next critical phase of spiritual formation—alignment with divine purpose. Just as Noah opened the window after forty days to glimpse the next steps of his journey, today, we look at another powerful biblical moment where forty signifies preparation and positioning for what's ahead.

By the time we met Isaac, the flood's purpose had been fulfilled, and mankind had moved forward in its journey. Many years had passed, and now a new covenantal lineage was unfolding. Interestingly, while the number forty is not explicitly highlighted in the story of Abraham, it appears in subtle but significant ways. During Abraham's famous intercession for Sodom, the negotiation moved in increments from fifty down to ten—a factor of forty embedded in the divine exchange (Genesis 18:22-33).

Moreover, God established circumcision as a symbol of His covenant, instructing Abraham to perform it on the eighth day—a factor of forty that signified divine consecration (Genesis 17:12). Abraham also received the prophecy that his descendants would endure four hundred years of slavery—a multiple of forty—foreshadowing a period of testing and formation (Genesis 15:13). Yet, it would be his son, Isaac, who would experience a direct manifestation of the number forty.

> *"And Isaac was forty years old when he took Rebekah to wife, the daughter of Bethuel the Syrian of Padanaram, the sister to Laban the Syrian."*
> ***(Genesis 25:20)***

Isaac's marriage to Rebekah was not a coincidence but a divinely coordinated event where every person involved played a crucial role. Abraham, understanding the weight of God's covenant, ensured that his son's future was aligned with divine promises. Instead of leaving Isaac's marriage to chance, he sent his most trusted servant on a mission to find a wife from his own people. This demonstrates that when God gives us a promise, we must actively prepare and position ourselves for its fulfillment.

The servant, entrusted with this great responsibility, did not rely on his own understanding but sought God in prayer. He asked for a clear sign, and before he had even finished praying, Rebekah appeared at the well, fulfilling every detail of his request. His immediate response was worship—acknowledging that God had led him to the right person. His example reminds us that when we seek God's direction, He is faithful to guide us.

Rebekah's role in this divine connection was just as significant. She was not searching for a new life, yet when the opportunity arose, she responded with remarkable faith. She left behind her home, her family, and all that was familiar to step into the unknown. Her willingness to trust in what God was doing, despite not knowing every detail, is a powerful display of faith and surrender.

Isaac, at forty years old, had waited patiently for the right person. When Rebekah arrived, he welcomed her as his wife without hesitation, fully embracing God's choice for him. His patience and trust in divine timing remind us that waiting on God always leads to the best outcomes.

This story is more than just a historical marriage account—it is a lesson in how God fulfills His purpose when we actively participate in His plan. Abraham's preparation, the servant's prayers, Rebekah's willingness, and Isaac's patience all played a part in bringing about God's promise. Whether we are in a season of preparation, seeking guidance, or stepping into the unknown, we must trust that God is working behind the scenes.

Reflection:

- In what areas of my life do I need to trust God's divine timing?
- Am I actively preparing for the promises I'm praying for?
- How can I align my actions with God's will, just as Isaac, Rebekah, and the servant did?

Affirmation:

I trust that God's timing is perfect. I am preparing my heart, aligning my actions, and stepping forward in faith. Like Isaac, I choose to wait on the Lord's best, knowing that He is orchestrating every detail for my good. My steps are ordered, my future is secured, and I embrace God's divine purpose for my life

DAY 6

THE INJURIES OF IMPULSIVENESS

Welcome to Day 6! You are progressing through this forty-day journey beautifully. Just as a fetus' limb buds, the foundation of the arms and legs, begin to form in physical development, spiritually, this is a time when movement starts to take shape in your journey. Arms symbolize action, and legs signify direction. Before you move, you must ensure that your steps are aligned with God's purpose. As we transition from Day 5, where we learned about God's divine timing in Isaac's life, today we look at the dangers of moving too quickly, stepping ahead without wisdom, and acting on impulse rather than faith.

Here goes forty again in the family! But this time, it is not a story of alignment like Isaac's. Instead, we see another example of forty marking a moment of significance, yet this one serves as a cautionary tale. Esau, at the age of forty, made a decision that was not in alignment with God's covenant. His choices were driven by impulse rather than wisdom, setting off a chain of consequences that he could not undo. As we reflect on his story, we are reminded of the importance of patience, discernment, and seeking God before making life-altering decisions.

> *"And Esau was forty years old when he took to wife Judith the daughter of Beeri the Hittite, and Bashemath the daughter of Elon the Hittite."*
> ***(Genesis 26:34)***

Isaac and Esau had both reached forty, when they made marriage decisions, but their choices could not have been more different. Isaac waited, trusting in God's plan, and his servant sought divine guidance before choosing Rebekah, ensuring she was aligned with the covenant. Esau, on the other hand, rushed into marriage without regard for God's plan or his family's wisdom, marrying women who led him further away from his spiritual inheritance.

Esau's life was marked by impulsive decisions that carried long-term consequences. His marriages caused grief to his parents, Isaac and Rebekah, who understood the importance of keeping their lineage aligned with God's promise. If family gatherings with in-laws have ever been awkward, imagine the discomfort in Isaac's household with Esau's choices! He didn't just make a bad decision, he doubled it by taking two wives who were outside of God's covenant.

And, in classic Esau fashion, when he realized his mistake, he tried to "fix" it with yet another impulsive act—marrying a daughter of Ishmael, as if stacking poor decisions would somehow neutralize the first ones. Rather than pausing to seek God's direction, he repeated the same cycle: reaction instead of reflection, short-term solutions instead of lasting wisdom.

Esau's impulsiveness wasn't new. We saw it earlier when he traded his birthright for a bowl of stew, choosing immediate gratification over lasting inheritance. These repeated choices show how acting on impulse can injure not just our present circumstances but our entire future. His story is a stark reminder that what feels urgent in the moment can lead to regret when viewed in hindsight.

Decisions made in haste, without prayer or discernment, can cause wounds that take years to heal. Impulsiveness may offer quick satisfaction, but it often comes at the cost of long-term regret. Instead of reacting to emotions or circumstances, we must learn to pause, pray, and pursue wisdom. Your limb buds are forming; your spiritual movement is beginning. Before you act, ensure that your direction is aligned with God's will. He desires that we seek Him first, trusting that His way is always better than our fleeting desires.

Reflection:

- Have I ever made impulsive decisions that resulted in regret or spiritual setbacks?
- Do I take time to seek God before making major life choices, or do I act based on emotions and pressure?
- How can I develop patience and spiritual discernment to avoid the injuries of impulsiveness?

Just as the limb buds in the womb will eventually form into strong, functional limbs, your ability to act wisely and walk in purpose is being shaped. Will you allow God to direct your steps, or will you rush ahead and stumble? Let this be a season where your movement is fortified by faith, not weakened by impulse.

Affirmation:

I choose wisdom over impulse, patience over haste. My steps are ordered by God, and I trust His divine timing. Like Isaac, I align myself with God's will, knowing that His plans lead to purpose and peace. I will not be swayed by fleeting emotions, but will stand firm in faith, allowing God to guide every decision I make.

DAY 7

Forget the Start—Focus on the Finish

Welcome to Day 7! Seven—the divine number of completion, God's perfect signature across creation. From the seven days of creation to the sevenfold Spirit of God (Revelation 1:4, 3:1, 4:5, and 5:6), this number signals wholeness, fulfillment, and the ultimate divine stamp of approval. Today, we reflect on something that transcends beginnings: the power of how we finish.

By now, you've been stretched, challenged, and perhaps even had a few lightbulb moments about your own patterns of faith and impulsiveness (thank you, Esau, for the cautionary tale). But today isn't about missteps or mishaps; it's about legacy—about leaving behind a life so well-lived that even those outside of your covenant community take notice. Because let's be honest, it's one thing for your family to grieve your passing, but when your former rivals mourn you too? That's another level of impact.

Jacob's life was nothing short of a divine drama. He began as the heel-grabbing trickster, wrestling his way through life—both figuratively and literally. Yet, by the end, he wasn't just a man of faith; he was a patriarch who commanded the respect of both the Israelites and the Egyptians. The Egyptians, mind you—the same people who would later enslave Jacob's descendants—took forty days to embalm him, ensuring his physical preservation in honor of his significance.

> *"And forty days were fulfilled for him; for so are fulfilled the days of those which are embalmed: and the Egyptians mourned for him threescore and ten days."* ***(Genesis 50:3)***

Forty days—again, the number of transition, of divine process. The Egyptians saw something in Jacob that warranted a time of mourning beyond their own customs. His life was not just significant to his immediate descendants but commanded the reverence of a foreign empire. This dual mourning period—forty days of embalming according to Egyptian practice and an additional thirty days of Hebrew mourning—underscored the weight of Jacob's journey. It was a life that started with deception but ended with honor.

Jacob's death was like a national holiday. This was likely because of Joseph's high status. Jacob was the father of the man who saved Egypt from famine, and his passing was marked with unprecedented honor. While the Egyptians mourned him for seventy days, the children of Israel mourned him for an additional seven days at Atad before his burial in Canaan (Genesis 50:10). This brought the total mourning period to seventy-seven days—a number reflecting deep reverence and recognition of Jacob's impact on history.

But what of Esau? His story, woven so tightly with Jacob's, was one of unfulfilled potential. The man who once held the birthright—the sacred, God-ordained promise—traded it away for a meal. A moment of hunger outweighed a lifetime of blessing. And that one impulsive act shaped everything that followed.

Let's compare this to another transition at forty: Esau's marriage at the same milestone. Unlike Isaac, who aligned himself with divine covenant, Esau took a path of impulse, marrying outside the faith and bringing grief to his family (Genesis 26:34-35). One man's forty signified wisdom and alignment; the other's marked a decision that pulled him further away from divine destiny. The contrast is glaring—one honored, one regretted. One finished well, the other struggled in bitterness. Esau, despite his potential, ended up displaced, seeking reconciliation far too late and lamenting what he had lost.

So, the question is: how do we ensure our forty marks transition into glory and not grief? It's not about how you start, but how you finish. Jacob, despite all his flaws, secured his legacy by ensuring the promises of Abraham remained intact. Esau, despite having every opportunity, allowed his choices to steer him away from his rightful place.

What about you? Are you living today in a way that future generations will honor? Are your choices positioning you for a finish that speaks of faith and fulfillment?

Reflection:

- Am I living in a way that ensures I finish well, leaving behind a legacy of faith and blessing?
- How do I respond to struggles and past mistakes—do they push me away from God or draw me closer?
- What practical steps can I take today to strengthen my faith and walk in divine alignment?

Affirmation:

I am not defined by my beginnings, but by my faithfulness to God's purpose. I choose to walk in alignment with His will, ensuring that my life reflects His promises. I will finish well, leaving behind a legacy of faith, honor, and divine fulfillment.

DAY 8

EXODUS—FORTY CHAPTERS FROM PHARAOH TO FREEDOM

Welcome to Day 8! The number eight signifies new beginnings and renewal—an opportunity to embrace God's divine reset within the cycles of forty.

On that note, are you ready for another forty to fortify your faith? Over the past few days, we've explored how God used the forty motif to shape the lives of Noah, Isaac, Esau, and Jacob. Now, prepare yourself for another transformative journey of forty.

Just as a developing embryo begins to form fingers and toes in week 8 of gestation, marking the early stages of its ability to grasp and walk, today we reflect on what we are reaching for and where we are headed spiritually. Are we reaching for

God's promises, or clinging to the familiarity of the past? Are we walking in faith, or stumbling in doubt?

The book of Exodus is unique, standing alone as the only book in the Bible with forty chapters. With its numerous references to forty, it is the 'headquarters' of this sacred number. This number, often linked to testing, transformation, and divine fulfillment, frames Israel's journey from bondage to worship.

The word "Exodus" means "a mass departure," a journey from one place to another. The book of Exodus captures this concept perfectly—not just as a physical movement, but as an emotional and spiritual journey as well. However, though Israel left Egypt in body, they remained attached to it in heart. Their longing for the past, even after being set free, shows that leaving a place is easier than leaving a mindset.

Exodus is more than history—it is a spiritual blueprint, showing how God delivers, establishes covenant, and calls us into His presence. For the next few days, we will focus on Moses and the Israelites, examining how they were forged, refined, and formed through cycles of forty in Exodus and beyond.

> *"Therefore, say to the Israelites: 'I am the LORD, and I will bring you out from under the yoke of the Egyptians. I will free you from being slaves to them, and I will redeem you with an outstretched arm and with mighty acts of judgment.'"*
> ***(Exodus 6:6)***

Exodus chronicles Israel's journey from slavery in Egypt, where they suffered for four hundred years. In their distress, they cried out to God, and He heard them. He raised up Moses—a man with a past, a man with doubts, but a man chosen for a divine mission. Through ten plagues, God displayed His power over Egypt's gods, culminating in the Passover. Covered by the blood of the lamb, Israel walked into freedom.

But freedom was just the beginning. Their journey led them to the Red Sea—a test of faith where God parted the waters, allowing them to cross on dry ground, leaving Egypt behind. Yet Egypt remained in their hearts. In the wilderness, they doubted, complained, and longed for the familiarity of their former bondage. How often do we also yearn for the comfort of old chains instead of stepping fully into God's plan?

At Mount Sinai, God called them into covenant. His goal was not just to rescue them but to be their God. He gave them His laws, shaping them into a set-apart people. Yet, even as Moses spent forty days with God, the people turned to idolatry, crafting a golden calf to replace the unseen God. How often do we trade His presence for something tangible but empty?

Despite their failures, God remained faithful. He did not abandon them but provided instructions for the Tabernacle—His dwelling place among them. Exodus does not conclude with their rebellion but with God's glory filling the Tabernacle, a sign that He was still leading them.

Exodus is our story. What areas of our lives require an exodus? Have we physically left situations but remained emotionally bound? Have we stepped into freedom, yet still act as though we are enslaved? God has delivered us, but do we trust Him? He has called us into relationship, but will we obey? He invites us into His presence, but will we enter? The journey to freedom is more than escape—it is about worship, trust, and walking with God.

For the next few days, we will explore all the forties captured in the book of Exodus, uncovering how God used this number to shape His people and deepen their dependence on Him. Likewise, we are in earth's final Exodus—a spiritual journey where we are being called out of this world's bondage, preparing to enter the ultimate Promised Land. Just as the Israelites wandered before reaching Canaan, we, too, are journeying through trials, trusting that one day, we will step into the fullness of God's eternal kingdom.

Reflection:

- What is my Egypt? Is there a place, habit, or mindset God has freed me from, yet I struggle to leave behind?
- Do I trust God fully, or do I long for old comforts in times of difficulty?
- Am I seeking God only for deliverance, or am I truly pursuing His presence?
- If my life were written in forty chapters, would it end in the promised land, or would I still be wandering in the wilderness?

Affirmation:

I am on a divine journey, called out of bondage and into freedom. I will not look back to Egypt, but I will move forward in faith. God has delivered me, and I trust Him to lead me to His promises. I walk in obedience, embrace transformation, and seek His presence above all else. My Exodus is not just an escape—it is an entry into His purpose for my life.

DAY 9

EMBRACING GOD'S TIMING—THE DANGER OF MOVING TOO SOON

Welcome to Day 9! Yesterday, we marveled at the book of Exodus—the powerful account of deliverance, covenant, and transformation of the Israelites who journeyed from bondage through the wilderness toward the Promised Land. Now, we turn our focus to the man who led that exodus—Moses. Before he could lead God's people out, he had to undergo his own exodus—one of preparation, waiting, and learning to trust God's timing.

Moses' life followed a structured rhythm of forty-year phases, each serving as a distinct season of preparation. Among all biblical figures, he experienced the most profound fulfillment and strengthening through forty. He lived for 120 years, divided into three sets of forty: forty years in Pharaoh's palace, forty years in the wilderness of Midian, and forty years leading the Israelites to the Promised Land. One might even call him the 'foreman of forty'—a leader shaped by this sacred number. Over the next few days, we will explore these cycles, uncovering and extracting the lessons for our fortification.

The number forty consistently represents refinement, testing, and preparation, marking pivotal moments of transformation and renewal in the lives of God's people. But today, we focus on another critical aspect—timing. Moses' first forty years were a period of preparation, but his impatience led to a costly mistake. His story reminds us that moving ahead of God can create unnecessary detours.

Today, we learn the value of trusting His process.

> *"When Moses was forty years old, it came into his heart to visit his brothers, the children of Israel...And seeing one of them suffer wrong, he defended and avenged him who was oppressed...But the next day, he appeared to two of them as they were fighting, and tried to reconcile them, saying, 'Men, you are brothers. Why do you wrong one another?'"*
> ***(Acts 7:23-30)***

Moses' first forty years were marked by privilege, growing up as a prince in Pharaoh's palace, yet his heart was always with the oppressed Israelites. At forty, feeling a deep sense of responsibility, he acted impulsively to defend his people. Seeing an Egyptian mistreating an Israelite, he struck the man down and buried him in the sand, believing his action would initiate Israel's deliverance.

However, when he attempted to mediate a dispute between two Israelites the next day, they rejected his authority, asking, "Who made you ruler over us?" Realizing his actions had been exposed, Moses fled to the wilderness.

This moment—burying the Egyptian in the sand—teaches a crucial lesson: when we rush ahead of God, we often find ourselves covering our mistakes. Moses' attempt to fulfill his calling in his own strength led to confusion, fear, and ultimately, exile. By attempting to take matters into his own hands, he delayed God's plan instead of stepping into it with patience and trust. Moving ahead of God's timing often creates unnecessary struggles that could have been avoided through patience and faith.

Moses' first forty years reveal that God's timing is essential. His intentions were noble, but his actions were premature. Only when Moses learned to wait for God's direction did he fully embrace his divine calling.

The question is: Are you willing to wait, or will impatience lead you down an unnecessary detour?

Reflection:

- Have you ever rushed ahead of God, trying to fix things in your own strength?
- What consequences have you faced because of acting impulsively?
- How can you grow in trusting God's timing and seeking His guidance before making decisions?

Like Moses, we often rush ahead of God when we think we know the way, but His timing is always better. Today, take time to reflect on how you can trust God more fully and wait for His direction in your life.

Affirmation:

I choose to trust in God's perfect timing. I will not move ahead of Him, but will wait with patience and faith. My steps are ordered by the Lord, and I embrace His process of preparation. I surrender my plans to His wisdom, knowing that He will lead me into His best for my life.

DAY 10

MOSES' MIDIAN MISSION

It's Day 10! Congrats, you are now a fetus! Just as a fetus transitions from an embryo and its vital organs begin to function, your spiritual journey is also entering a phase of greater development. What was once forming is now active, purposeful, and sustaining life. This parallels Moses' second forty-year cycle—a time of obscurity, waiting, and preparation. It may have seemed like he had been cast aside, but beneath the surface, God was shaping a leader.

Moses had begun with power and privilege in Pharaoh's palace, but one impulsive decision sent him into exile. Yet, what appeared to be a setback was actually God's strategy to equip him for his ultimate purpose. Are you in a season where you feel hidden or sidelined? Just as the transformation from an embryo to a fetus is imperceptible outside the mother's body, we will discover that God often does His most outstanding work in us when no one is watching.

> *"When Moses heard this, he fled to Midian, where he settled as a foreigner and had two sons. After forty years had passed, an angel appeared to him in the flames of a burning bush in the desert near Mount Sinai."*
> ***(Acts 7:29-30)***

After Moses fled Egypt, he found himself in Midian, far from the life of influence he had once known. For forty years, he worked as a shepherd for his father-in-law, Jethro. This was not a punishment—it was a divine season of preparation. Midian became the training ground where Moses was shaped, refined, and made ready to lead. It was in Midian that Moses encountered the burning bush, the moment that set fire to his divine calling.

In Midian, Moses also met his wife, Zipporah, and started a family. Family life grounded him, shaping his character, teaching him patience, responsibility, and selflessness. His role as a husband and father helped prepare him to shepherd an entire nation.

Moses had acted impulsively in Egypt, trying to deliver his people in his own strength. But in Midian, God used this season to retrain and refine him. Here, Moses learned patience, humility, and dependence on God. Hidden from the world's view, God was preparing him for the world's stage. He grew in wisdom and understanding, learning to lead not by force, but by faith. His encounter with Jethro, who later advised him on delegation and leadership, helped him develop the ability to trust others and structure his leadership wisely.

We often experience seasons that feel like Midian—times of waiting, working behind the scenes, or feeling unseen. It's easy to believe nothing is happening, but God is always at work. Just as God used Moses' time in Midian to prepare him for his calling, He uses our waiting seasons to prepare us for what's next. Your spiritual "vital organs"—faith, perseverance, and wisdom—are forming and strengthening. This is your preparation phase.

Like Moses, you may find yourself in a 'Midian' season, feeling distanced from impact or recognition. But God often does His most profound work in the unseen places. He is refining, equipping, and preparing you. Every lesson, skill, and experience you gain now has a purpose in your future calling.

And let's be real—Moses probably didn't wake up every morning in Midian, look around at the sheep, and say, "Ah yes, this is precisely the glamorous leadership training I envisioned." But isn't that just like God? Taking the most unexpected places, the quietest seasons, and using them to shape world changers. If Moses had LinkedIn back then, his career trajectory would have looked wild: *Prince of Egypt → Fugitive → Shepherd → Nation Deliverer*. But God knew exactly what He was doing. And He knows what He's doing with you, too.

Reflection:

- What qualities or lessons do you think God is developing in you right now?
- How can you trust God more deeply during times of waiting and preparation?
- In what ways can you maximize your current season instead of resenting it?

Just as Moses' time in Midian was a season of preparation for his greater purpose, your waiting seasons are also times for God to refine you. Trust that He is working in you, even when you can't see the full picture. Embrace this process, for it will lead to growth and greater purpose.

Affirmation:

I trust that God is using my waiting season to refine and prepare me. I will not despise the process, but will embrace it, knowing He is strengthening me for the future. My time in obscurity is not wasted—it is a divine setup for the calling ahead. I walk forward in faith, knowing that nothing is wasted in God's hands.

DAY 11

MOSES' MANNA MISSION

Welcome to Day 11! You're making it through this journey, step by step—kind of like the Israelites, except with fewer sandstorms and way more snack options.

Yesterday, we wandered through Moses' years in Midian, where he mastered the arts of wilderness survival, sheep whispering, and divine patience. Every trial prepared him for what was to come—leading an entire nation through the desert. Now, as he stepped into his final forty-year cycle, all those lessons were about to be put to the ultimate test.

This marks the beginning of Moses' third forty-year season, which—surprise, surprise—coincided with forty years of Israelite wandering. A journey that should have taken mere weeks stretched into four decades due to their doubt, disobedience, and an impressive ability to miss the point entirely. We'll dive deeper into the consequences of their choices in the next chapter, but today, let's talk about God's grace—a grace that fell daily from heaven in the form of manna.

> *"Moses was eighty years old and Aaron eighty-three when they spoke to Pharaoh."*
> ***(Exodus 7:7)***

Moses, now stepping fully into his divine assignment, faced Pharaoh, led Israel out of slavery, and watched as the Red Sea made way for their escape. But freedom was only the beginning. The wilderness awaited—a place of testing, training, and total dependence on God.

For forty years, God provided manna from heaven, miraculously sustaining His people.

> *"The Israelites ate manna forty years, until they came to a land that was settled; they ate manna until they reached the border of Canaan."*
> ***(Exodus 16:35)***

They didn't farm it, bake it, or earn it—it was simply there, fresh each morning, a tangible reminder of God's faithfulness. The daily collection of manna wasn't just a survival tactic—it was a spiritual lesson. Would they trust God for their daily bread, or would they hoard in fear?

Despite their endless complaints (and they complained a lot), God remained faithful. He didn't cut off their food supply even when they grumbled about missing Egyptian buffets. When they craved meat, God provided quail—manna in the morning, quail in the evening (Exodus 16:13). But later, when they grew tired of manna and demanded more meat, their complaints turned into rebellion. God gave them what they asked for—an overwhelming amount of quail—but it came as a judgment. Those who greedily indulged in excess were struck with a plague (Numbers 11:31-34). And yet, even after this sobering lesson, manna remained their primary provision until they reached the Promised Land.

An interesting pattern emerged in how God provided the manna. It fell every morning, except on the seventh day. On the sixth day, they were instructed to gather a double portion so they could rest on the Sabbath (Exodus 16:22-26). This was a significant moment in establishing sacred ordinances, showing that even provision was structured around God's divine order. The lesson? Trust God's rhythm. He provides not only for our daily needs but also for our future rest. Those who ignored His instructions and went out to gather on the seventh day found nothing—further proving that God's plan is always best.

What's the lesson in all this?

1. **Be careful what you crave.** Sometimes, in our dissatisfaction, we long for things that are not meant to sustain us. The Israelites had supernatural provision, yet they rejected it for fleeting desires.

2. **God's provision is always intentional.** He provides what we need, not always what we want. Learning to appreciate what He gives is key to spiritual maturity.

3. **Trust in God's process and rhythm.** Just because we tire of the way He provides does not mean He is failing us—it means He is teaching us reliance, gratitude, and contentment.

Like the Israelites, we often stress over the "what ifs" of tomorrow, forgetting that God provides for today. Gathering manna required faith. It was a daily act of trust, just as our reliance on God must be daily, not occasional. The manna didn't last forever, though.

> *"The manna stopped the day after they ate the food from the land; there was no longer any manna for the Israelites, but that year they ate the produce of Canaan."*
> ***(Joshua 5:12)***

This transition marked a shift in how God provided. There was a time for miraculous provision and a time to step into what He had already prepared. God provides in different ways in different seasons. Sometimes, He rains down provision when we least expect it. Other times, He calls us to step into the land He has given us and cultivate what He has provided. Either way, He remains faithful. The question is: Are we willing to trust Him for what we need today, and are we ready to step into what He has for us tomorrow?

Reflection:

Take a moment to sit quietly and reflect on God's daily provision. Allow yourself to rest in the assurance that He sees and cares for your needs.

- In what ways has God provided for you daily, even when you didn't recognize it?
- Are you trusting God for your daily needs, or do you find yourself worrying about the future?
- How can you develop a habit of gratitude for God's continuous provision in your life?
- Just as the Israelites had to gather manna daily, how can you intentionally seek spiritual nourishment each day?

- Are you craving something that God has not appointed for you in this season? How can you realign your desires with His will?
- How do you observe rest? Do you trust that God has already made provision for your needs, even in seasons when you must pause and wait?

Affirmation:

I trust in God's daily provision. I will not fear for tomorrow, for He is faithful today. Like manna from heaven, His grace is fresh every morning, and His supply never runs dry. I receive what He provides with gratitude, knowing that whether in the wilderness or the Promised Land, He sustains me. I will not crave what He has not appointed for me, but I will trust in His perfect plan. I rest in His provision, knowing that He provides not just for today but also for the seasons to come. I walk in confidence, trusting in His unfailing care.

DAY 12

Doomed by Doubt: The 40-Day Scout

Welcome to Day 12! Your sensory systems—hearing, taste, and touch—are beginning to function at this stage. Your ability to perceive and respond to God's voice, His promises, and His direction is developing.

So, we have settled in the wilderness. You are in for a ride. Over the past few days, we have reflected on how God sustained His people, providing manna each morning and quail each evening. We've seen how His provision followed divine order—manna every day except the Sabbath, with a double portion given on the sixth day as a sacred ordinance of trust and obedience. Yet, even with this constant, miraculous provision, doubt still took root among the Israelites.

You would think they would trust God by now, right? Wrong! At this stage in their journey, the Israelites were supposed to have sharpened their spiritual senses to recognize and trust in

God's promises. Yet, instead of tuning into faith, they allowed fear to dictate their response. They doubted His promise, provision, and protection, leading them to spend forty days scouting a land that was already theirs for the taking.

God intended for them to go through the wilderness for a short time of refinement before bringing them into the Promised Land. But after two years, doubt crept in when they reached the border, and they asked Moses to send spies to scout the land. From a human perspective, this seemed logical, but it displeased God because He had already promised them victory. Their lack of faith resulted in a forty-year sentence of wandering. Today, we reflect on the spies' 40-day mission and the cost of doubting God's promise before exploring how doubt delayed the Israelites' journey in the next chapter.

> *"At the end of forty days they returned from exploring the land."*
> ***(Numbers 13:25)***

After forty days of exploring Canaan, the twelve spies returned with a report. What should have been a moment of triumph, filled with anticipation, turned into fear, doubt, and rebellion. Ten of the spies focused on the obstacles—the giants and the fortified cities. They saw the land as one that "devours those living in it" and exaggerated the threats. Their conclusion? The challenges were too great.

But Caleb and Joshua had a different perspective. They saw the same land but through the lens of faith. Caleb boldly declared, "We should go up and take possession of the land, for we can certainly do it." He wasn't blind to the giants, but he knew that with God, they could overcome. Sadly, the negative report spread, fear took over, and the people refused to move forward. Their hesitation cost them the Promised Land.

The story of the twelve spies is a powerful reminder that our spiritual perception determines our response. The ten spies allowed fear to distort their view and dictate their actions, leading to rebellion and missed opportunities. But Caleb and Joshua focused on God's promises, believing in His power over their obstacles. Their faith positioned them for victory.

The lesson is clear: fear dulls our spiritual senses and stalls our progress, while faith sharpens our perception and moves us toward God's promises. Sometimes, what appears to be the logical path is actually a detour from God's best plan for us. The Israelites believed scouting the land would give them reassurance, but instead, it led them deeper into doubt and disobedience. Doubt weakens our faith and redirects us toward human reasoning, causing us to miss out on the blessings God has already secured for us.

We all face giants—situations that seem impossible to overcome. Whether it's financial struggles, relationship difficulties, or personal challenges, fear can paralyze us. But just like Caleb and Joshua, we have a choice: focus on the giants, or focus on the God who is greater than every obstacle.

Just as sensory systems allow us to experience and respond to the world, our faith must be trained to discern God's voice, trust His leading, and respond in obedience. The Israelites had every reason to believe God was with them, but they failed to taste and see that the Lord is good. Instead of trusting what they had already heard and seen, they allowed doubt to dull their spiritual senses.

The question is: What are you tuning into—faith or fear? Are your spiritual senses developing in alignment with God's Word, or are they being dulled by doubt?

Reflection:

- What giants in my life am I currently focused on, and how is my perspective affecting my actions?
- In what areas have I allowed fear to dictate my decisions instead of trusting in God's promises?
- How can I shift my focus from the challenges in front of me to the God who is greater than all my fears?
- Am I gathering and trusting God's daily provision, or am I doubting that He will provide for my next step?

Doubt has the power to magnify problems and minimize God's promises. The ten spies saw the same land as Caleb and Joshua, but instead of seeing opportunity, they saw opposition. When we trust in what we see instead of who God is, we forfeit the victories He has already secured for us. Today, choose to trust in God's word, step forward in faith, and refuse to let doubt dictate your destiny. Faith doesn't dismiss challenges; it sees them through the lens of God's power and trusts in His ability to overcome them. Just as Caleb and Joshua focused on God's promises instead of obstacles, we too can shift our focus from fear to faith and walk boldly into our promised victories.

Affirmation:

I choose to trust in God's promises rather than fear the giants before me. My faith is being sharpened, and my spiritual senses are attuned to His voice. I will not allow doubt to dull my vision or delay my destiny. I walk forward with confidence, knowing that what God has promised, He will fulfill. I am stepping into the land He has given me, fully assured that He is greater than any obstacle in my path.

DAY 13

THE 40-YEAR PUNISHMENT

Welcome to Day 13! Yesterday, we watched in frustration as the Israelites let fear rob them of their promise. Today, we dive into the consequences of their doubt—how their hesitation led to a forty-year delay that could have been avoided. If you've ever made a decision that had you wandering in circles, you might relate.

The Israelites stood on the edge of their promise, but fear and murmuring consumed them. Though they had physically left Egypt, their minds were still in chains. Instead of seeing themselves as conquerors, they shrank into grasshopper mode—small, weak, and incapable of victory, despite having a God who had just parted an entire sea for them. Their unwillingness to trust Him revealed a deep-seated disbelief that angered God.

> *"And your children shall wander in the wilderness forty years, and bear your whoredoms, until your carcasses be wasted in the wilderness. After the number of the days in which ye searched the land, even forty days, each day for a year, shall ye bear your iniquities, even forty years, and ye shall know my breach of promise."* ***(Numbers 14:33-34)***

God was ready to wipe them out entirely. Enter Moses—the ultimate intercessor. He pleaded with God, reminding Him of His covenant and asking for mercy. God relented, but the consequence remained—forty years of wandering as judgment for their forty days of doubt. One day of fear equaled one year of delay. If procrastination had a mascot, it would be this moment in history.

Yet, even in this punishment, there was mercy. Though they rebelled, God still provided manna, sustained their clothes and sandals, and led them with His presence. He didn't abandon them; He disciplined them. His judgment was not meant to destroy them, but to correct and refine them, giving the next generation a chance to succeed where their ancestors had failed.

But make no mistake—forty years is a long time. An entire generation lived and died in the wilderness. The years passed, and with them, so did those who clung to the old mindset. It took a long time for the chains of Egypt to disappear from their hearts. During this time, life still happened. Babies were born. The elderly were buried. Weddings were celebrated, anniversaries marked, and birthdays acknowledged. They worshiped, held court, and developed new customs and cultures. Their identity as a people was reshaped, yet many still held on to their wilderness mentality, never fully embracing the promises ahead.

How many of us have been wandering in cycles for years? How many of us have been spiritually stuck, circling the same mountains of doubt, fear, and disobedience, while our promise is just within reach? Some of us are a few steps, maybe a few weeks, away from breakthrough, yet we keep encircling the same obstacles because we refuse to let go of old chains. The Israelites could see the Promised Land, but their hearts and habits kept them wandering.

If God is leading you somewhere, don't take the scenic route of doubt. Trust Him, step forward, and avoid unnecessary wandering!

Reflection:

- Are murmuring and doubt delaying my progress?
- What habits or attitudes do I need to surrender to God?

- How is God using this season to prepare me for His promises?
- Am I holding onto an old mindset that is keeping me from trusting God fully?
- What cycles have I been stuck in, and what steps can I take to break free?

The Israelites' punishment was not just about time—it was about trust. Their unbelief nearly cost them everything, but Moses interceded on their behalf. Even in judgment, God showed mercy. Are you prolonging your wilderness season by doubting God? Choose faith today, break free from the old mindset, and walk confidently into His promises.

Affirmation:

I will not let doubt keep me circling the same mountains. I trust God's timing, His plan, and His promises. My past will not define my future. I break free from fear, complacency, and hesitation. I am stepping boldly into my promise, knowing that God has already made the way. My wilderness season is not my final destination—I am moving forward in faith.

DAY 14

THE 40-DAY REVELATION

Welcome to Day 14! You are doing great! By now, your faith is strengthening, your spiritual discernment is sharpening, and your understanding of God's ways is deepening. Much like a growing body develops distinct features, your spiritual identity is becoming clearer. Your spiritual bones are hardening, giving you structure. Your face is taking shape, reflecting the character of Christ. Your heart, liver, kidneys, and other essential organs are functioning, filtering what is necessary and removing what is not. In the same way, your faith must mature, your discernment must take form, and your ability to process truth must be sharpened.

For days, we have explored themes of purpose, preparation, provision, and purging. But there is something deeper that sustains and guides all of these—dwelling in God's presence. Throughout scripture, God calls His people not only to obedience but to intimate fellowship with Him. Moses experienced this in a profound way when he ascended Mount Sinai for forty days and forty nights. There, separated from the distractions below, he encountered God in a way that changed not just his own life but the destiny of an entire nation.

> *"And Moses went into the midst of the cloud, and gat him up into the mount: and Moses was in the mount forty days and forty nights."*
> ***(Exodus 24:18)***

This was not just a moment of receiving the Law—it was a divine revelation. Moses did not just go up to collect stone tablets; he went up to meet with God. His first forty-day trek up the mountain was where God gave him instructions on how the people were to worship Him. It was there, in the presence of God, that he received divine direction—not just for the nation but for himself. When we dwell in God's presence, that is where we receive instruction for our personal walk. That is where we learn to worship Him in spirit and in truth.

Yet, while Moses was immersed in divine revelation, the people below were spiritually disconnected. Impatient, restless, and unwilling to wait, they created an idol to worship—a man-made substitute for the God who had just miraculously delivered them. Their actions reveal a dangerous reality: when we do not seek God for ourselves, we are tempted to follow the voices of the crowd. Too often, we rely on secondhand encounters—hot-spotting from other people's faith—rather than developing a personal relationship with God. But God is calling us higher. He is calling us to seek Him, not just through the experiences of others, but through an intimate, personal pursuit.

Much like a process of refining gold, what is forming in us determines what we will become. If impatience and rebellion shape us, we may be spiritually malnourished when we step into our purpose. But if we choose to dwell in God's presence, we are fortified for the journey ahead.

How often do we do the same as the Israelites? Instead of waiting in God's presence, do we try to force our own answers? Instead of trusting His timing, do we grow restless and settle for lesser things? Revelation requires relationship, and that means making space for God—not just in moments of desperation, but in daily pursuit. A true encounter with God will reshape our thoughts, refine our hearts, and align us with His will.

Moses' time in God's presence left him with more than instructions—it left him with transformation. Likewise, what will be different about you after this journey? Will your faith be stronger? Will your discernment be sharper? Will you emerge fortified and transformed, or will you, like the

Israelites, be distracted by the temporary? The choice is yours.

Reflection:

- Do I intentionally set time aside to dwell in God's presence?
- What distractions do I need to remove to hear from Him more clearly?
- Am I seeking His presence or just His answers?
- Have I been relying on the spiritual experiences of others rather than developing my own relationship with God?

Like Moses, you are invited to dwell in God's presence, not just for instruction but for transformation. God is waiting to reveal His plans, shape your heart, and lead you into greater purpose—but you must make space to hear Him. Will you ascend the mountain?

Affirmation:

I will dwell in God's presence, not just for instruction, but for transformation. I will not rely on secondhand encounters but will seek Him for myself. As I make space for God in my life, I receive divine direction, wisdom, and revelation. My faith is deepening, my discernment is sharpening, and I am becoming all that God has called me to be. I walk in truth, worship in spirit, and remain steadfast in His presence.

DAY 15

40-DAYS OF RENEWAL AND RESTORATION

Welcome to Day 15! You are doing excellently! Today, you are officially fifteen days fortified, and what better way to celebrate than to explore the theme of renewal and restoration?

If yesterday taught us anything, it's that mountaintop experiences don't exempt us from valley battles. Moses had just spent forty days marinating in divine glory, only to descend into a golden calf rave gone horribly wrong. One moment, he's holding the very laws of God—etched by His own hand—and the next, he's hurling them to the ground in sheer disbelief. Talk about a dramatic exit. But here's the thing—God wasn't done writing His story with Israel, and He wasn't done with Moses either.

After every spiritual triumph comes testing, trials, and temptations. The enemy doubled his efforts the moment

Moses returned. What greeted him was so disturbing that he literally broke God's laws. The shattered tablets symbolized the fractured covenant, but the story does not end there. God called Moses back to the mountain for a second forty-day encounter—not just to rewrite the law, but to restore what was broken. Today, we explore the idea of temptation after a spiritual encounter, how to return to God after failure, and how seeking His presence through fasting and prayer leads to true renewal.

> *"And it came to pass, as soon as he came nigh unto the camp, that he saw the calf, and the dancing: and Moses' anger waxed hot, and he cast the tables out of his hands, and brake them beneath the mount."*
> ***(Exodus 32:19-20)***
>
> *"And he was there with the Lord forty days and forty nights; he did neither eat bread, nor drink water: and he wrote upon the tables the words of the covenant, the ten commandments."*
> ***(Exodus 34:28)***

Moses' journey is a reflection of our own. Often, after we have experienced a deep encounter with God—whether through prayer, fasting, or personal revelation—the enemy comes swiftly to challenge what we have received. We may find ourselves tested, tempted, and even discouraged. Like Moses, we return from spiritual highs only to face opposition, setbacks, and struggles. The Israelites' rebellion was not just an act of impatience—it was a test that exposed their flickering faith.

Moses teaches us what to do in these moments: return for more time with God. Instead of dwelling in frustration or giving up, he ascended the mountain again. This second encounter was different—when Moses came back, he glowed with the glory of God. His face radiated the evidence of dwelling in God's presence. This transformation was not just an external change but a symbol of the renewal and restoration that comes when we refuse to let failure define us.

What do we do when trials come after spiritual victories? We return to the presence of God. We fast, pray, and press in again. The key to overcoming temptation, discouragement, and spiritual fatigue is not in retreating but in pursuing more of God. When we seek Him after the struggle, we not only regain what was lost—we shine with His glory.

Reflection:

- In what ways have I been tested after a spiritual breakthrough?
- How can I respond like Moses—by returning to God rather than giving up?

- What does it mean for me to "glow" with the evidence of God's presence in my life?

Moses didn't stop at frustration—he returned to the mountain and came back transformed. Likewise, when we face opposition, we must seek God even more. And when we do, we won't return the same—we will glow with the evidence of His presence. Will you ascend the mountain again?

Affirmation:

I will not let trials shake my faith or setbacks define me. When challenges come, I will return to God's presence for renewal and restoration. I am strengthened, fortified, and transformed by His glory. I do not retreat—I ascend. I do not surrender—I seek Him even more. His presence is my refuge, and in Him, I am made whole.

DAY 16

Knowing When to Let Go—The Power of Transition

Welcome to Day 16! You're looking fortified and faith-filled after yesterday's glow-up from time spent in God's presence. Can you imagine how transformed you will be by the end of this journey? The wilderness is closing, but the mission isn't over. Moses has completed his course, and Israel stands at the threshold of a new era. What's next?

At sixteen weeks of pregnancy, the mother's body is making major shifts. The uterus is expanding, the baby bump is becoming more visible, and increased energy levels return. Weight gain is noticeable, and the breasts begin producing colostrum in preparation for nourishment. The round ligaments stretch, causing discomfort, and a dark line, the linea nigra, appears down the center of the abdomen. These changes indicate that the body is preparing for something greater. In the same way, Israel was stretching, shifting, and visibly transforming. No longer hidden in the wilderness, they were preparing to step into their next phase of destiny. They would no longer feed on manna but on milk and honey (Exodus 3:8). No longer would they travel in circles—they would walk a straight path through the Jordan into the Promised Land.

Moses, the champion of the mission, had lived through three cycles of forty—a life structured by divine order. From forty years in Pharaoh's palace to forty years in Midian, and finally, forty years leading the Israelites through the wilderness, his journey was complete. He had finished his race, and though he would not enter the Promised Land, his impact was undeniable.

> *"Moses was a hundred and twenty years old when he died, yet his eyes were not weak nor his strength gone."* ***(Deuteronomy 34:7)***

One hundred and twenty—three forties—a number marking both the culmination of leadership and the transition into something new. It mirrored the 120-year warning given in Noah's time (Genesis 6:3), signaling a generational shift and a divine reset. The wilderness chapter was closing, but Israel's journey wasn't over. Moses still had the strength to keep going, but he accepted the close of his chapter. He did not enter the Promised Land, but he received a higher honor—God Himself buried him.

> *"And He buried him in a valley in the land of Moab, opposite Beth Peor; but no one knows his grave to this day."*
> ***(Deuteronomy 34:6)***

If Moses had social media, his final post might have read: "*120 years of service. Retiring early. Please respect my privacy. – Deuteronomy 34:7.*" He may not have crossed over, but he had fulfilled his purpose.

Moses' transition was not one of weakness but divine honor. His leadership was not about personal achievement but about preparing the next generation to walk into their destiny. The Israelites who had doubted were gone, their bones resting in the wilderness, while the faithful stood on the brink of their future.

There's a time to fight, to lead, to push forward—but there's also a time to release, to pass the mantle, and to accept when a season has ended. Even when we have the strength and will to continue, wisdom teaches us to recognize transitions. Moses understood this.

How many of us struggle to close chapters, even when we know a season has ended?

We see this in many aspects of life:

- A young adult must release their teenage years to step into maturity.
- A parent must let go as their child grows into independence.
- A career shift may demand that we leave behind a familiar role for a new opportunity.
- Relationships, friendships, and commitments change, and sometimes, we must release what once was.
- Even in ministry, there comes a time to train others and step aside for the next generation to lead.

It was now Joshua's moment. Moses had passed the mantle to Joshua through a formal commissioning by God and public laying on of hands to confer authority. Joshua was ready. Unlike Moses, his life was not framed by forties, but he understood the weight of forty. He had scouted the Promised Land for forty days and seen firsthand the cost of disobedience. Unlike Moses, who was trained in Midian, Joshua's leadership training was a forty-year marathon in the wilderness. He had seen rebellion bury an entire generation, witnessed miracles sustain the faithful, and learned that obedience was the key to entering the promise. His preparation had not been in palaces or private encounters with God on mountaintops—it had been in the daily grind of survival, discipline, and endurance. Now, he stood as the bridge between what was and what would be.

How many of us are standing at a transition point, still carrying the weight of old cycles? How many of us have been circling the same mountains, prolonging our wilderness journey when the promise is within view? The shift is here. The wilderness was never meant to be permanent—it was preparation for promise. Will you step into it?

Reflection:

- Am I holding onto old patterns that are keeping me from stepping into my promise?
- How can I shift my perspective to trust God fully in times of transition?
- Have I been circling the same mountains, delaying my breakthrough?
- Am I preparing those who will come after me, ensuring that faith continues beyond my lifetime?
- What lessons can I learn from previous generations so I don't repeat their mistakes?
- What season in my life is God calling me to close so I can step into the next?

Moses may not have entered the Promised Land, but he left behind a leader, a legacy, and a lesson: *Trust God, or you'll spend your days circling mountains meant to be crossed.*

Affirmation:

I embrace the shift that God is calling me into. I will not delay my promise with doubt, fear, or hesitation. I release old cycles, step forward in faith, and trust in God's perfect timing. Like Moses, I will recognize when a season has ended and accept God's new direction. Like Joshua, I am being trained for greater, and I will walk boldly into the inheritance God has prepared for me. My transition is not just about leaving but about stepping into something greater.

DAY 17

40 Years of Peace

Welcome to Day 17 and a new era! After watching the Israelites stumble through forty years of wandering (with an impressive track record of complaining), we finally arrive at a refreshing shift—forty years of peace. Can you imagine? No plagues, no rebellion, no last-minute golden calf disasters. Just rest. If the Israelites had a social media account back then, this would've been the ultimate "soft life" era.

> *"So the land had peace for forty years, until Othniel son of Kenaz died."*
> ***(Judges 3:11)***

Othniel, the first judge of Israel, led the nation into its first forty-year stretch of peace after entering the Promised Land. Picture it: going from decades of desert drama to forty years of serenity—an upgrade that only faithfulness to God could provide. If Israel had understood earlier that obedience leads to peace, they might have avoided a whole lot of detours (and sand in uncomfortable places).

After Joshua's death, the Israelites fell into their classic pattern—rebellion, oppression, regret, and desperate cries for help. Instead of learning from past mistakes, they did what they did best: forget God's goodness and land themselves in trouble. But when they finally came to their senses, God raised up Othniel, a courageous leader from the family of Caleb (a name we know and love from the spy mission days). With faith and boldness, Othniel led Israel to victory, breaking their cycle of suffering and ushering in a much-needed season of divine rest.

As a result of Othniel's leadership and faithfulness to God, the land enjoyed peace. And let's be honest—after years of wandering, war, and whining, the Israelites were probably relieved to put their battle gear down for a while. But this peace wasn't just a break from conflict; it was a tangible sign of God's favor. For the first time since stepping foot in the Promised Land, they could finally experience security, stability, and the freedom to worship without fear.

Othniel's story is a powerful reminder that obedience leads to peace. When we align our lives with God's will, we invite His presence into our circumstances. Othniel didn't just fight a battle—he set a foundation for an entire generation to experience peace. That means our choices today don't just affect us; they can shape the spiritual atmosphere for those who come after us.

This peace wasn't the result of perfect conditions; it was the result of walking in alignment with God. Just like Othniel's leadership secured Israel's peace, our trust in God can establish peace in our own hearts—even when chaos surrounds us. True peace isn't about having a stress-free life; it's about knowing who holds your life together. And let's be real, forty years of peace sounds like a pretty sweet deal for a little bit of obedience.

Reflection:

- When have I experienced God's peace in my life?
- Are there areas where I need to align myself more closely with God's will to experience His peace?
- How can I extend the peace God gives to those around me?
- What can I learn from the previous generation's mistakes to ensure I don't repeat them?
- Am I positioning myself to create a legacy of faith and peace for the next generation?

Othniel's obedience to God brought peace to an entire nation. When we choose to obey, even in small steps, we are creating an environment for peace to grow—not just in our own lives, but in the lives of those around us. Forty years of peace came after forty years of wandering—what will your next forty bring?

Affirmation:

I choose obedience, knowing that it leads to peace. I align my life with God's will and trust that His presence brings stability. I will not repeat cycles of fear and disobedience but will walk boldly in faith. As I follow God, I create a legacy of peace, not just for myself, but for those who come after me. My next forty will be filled with God's favor and divine rest.

DAY 18

COURAGE CONQUERS

Welcome to Day 18! After yesterday's peaceful reflection, today, we shift our focus to courage. Through this, we see that God loves the number forty, using it as a divine marker for fortification, growth, and victory. Each cycle of forty reveals a deeper lesson, and today, we discover how courage can transform not just individuals, but entire generations.

At eighteen weeks, movement is no longer just reflexive—a growing child can now kick, stretch, and even roll over with purpose. The once-subtle flutters are now unmistakable. Much like this stage of development, courage isn't just an abstract concept; it is a force that moves us, causes us to take action, and shifts the trajectory of our lives. Deborah's story is a perfect example of faith in motion—leading, guiding, and responding to God's call with confidence.

We saw how Othniel's leadership brought forty years of peace to Israel. However, after his death in 1302 BC, Israel once again fell into sin, triggering another cycle of oppression. This time, God allowed Eglon, king of Moab, to rule over them for eighteen years (Judges 3:12-14). But just as oppression seemed unending, God raised up Ehud, a left-handed Benjamite, who assassinated Eglon and led Israel to victory. This ushered in eighty years of peace—two consecutive forty-year cycles.

Yet, history repeated itself. After another period of disobedience, Israel found itself under twenty years of oppression, this time at the hands of King Jabin of Canaan. But as before, God was ready to raise a deliverer—one whose courage would break the cycle and restore Israel's peace for another forty years.

> *"So let all thine enemies perish, O Lord: but let them that love him be as the sun when he goeth forth in his might. And the land had rest forty years."*
> ***(Judges 5:31)***

In 1184 BC, Israel experienced another forty years of peace, secured through the bold leadership of Deborah and Barak. Their military success was pivotal, but the lasting peace that followed was rooted in something deeper—their faith and courage. They didn't rely on numbers or might; they relied on God.

Deborah's leadership was extraordinary in every way. As the first and only female judge of Israel, she stood in a position that few women held in ancient times. But she was not just a leader in title—she was a prophetess, a warrior, and a strategist. Her wisdom and authority were so widely respected that the Israelites came from all over to seek her judgment under the palm tree where she sat as a ruler and guide. When Israel was oppressed by King Jabin and his commander Sisera, it was Deborah who summoned Barak, giving him the charge to lead an army against their enemies. But Barak hesitated, insisting that he would only go if Deborah went with him. Without hesitation, Deborah agreed, but she boldly prophesied that because of his reluctance, the victory would not go to him, but to a woman.

That prophecy came to pass in an unexpected twist. As Sisera fled the battlefield in terror, he sought refuge in the tent of Jael, a seemingly harmless woman who welcomed him in, gave him milk, and let him rest. But as he slept, Jael took a tent peg and a hammer and drove the peg through his skull, delivering the final blow to Israel's enemy. Deborah's leadership and prophetic insight had not only rallied the nation but had also paved the way for an unexpected heroine to take part in the victory.

Much like an unborn child learning to stretch, move, and respond to the world beyond the womb, Deborah's story teaches us that courage is not passive—it is active, responsive, and intentional. She did not wait for someone else to step up;

she moved forward in faith. True courage is not the absence of fear but the willingness to act in obedience despite it.

The key takeaway from this story is that true victory comes when courage is combined with faith. It's not about having all the answers or being fearless—it's about stepping out in faith and trusting that God will lead the way, even when the path ahead is unclear. The forty-year victories in Israel's history serve as a reminder that courage doesn't just bring personal triumph—it can transform entire generations.

Reflection:

- When have you felt uncertain or fearful about stepping into something God has called you to do?
- How did your faith in Him give you courage in those moments?
- How can you shift your perspective from focusing on your fears to focusing on God's strength and faithfulness?
- In what areas of your life can you step forward with courage today, trusting that God will guide you?

Taking that first step of courage can be transformative. Like Deborah, we may not have all the answers, but by trusting God and stepping forward, we open ourselves to new possibilities and the strength He provides. Forty years of peace followed their courage—what victories could your courage bring?

Affirmation:

I choose courage over fear, faith over doubt, and action over hesitation. I trust that God has gone before me, preparing the way for victory. Like Deborah, I will lead with confidence, relying not on my strength but on God's power. My courage today will impact generations to come, and my obedience will bring lasting peace. I step forward boldly, knowing that when God calls, He also equips.

DAY 19

FROM WAVERING TO WARRIOR

Welcome to Day 19! Breathe! See how it feels when you are at peace? God's peace is the best medicine for the soul. Also, fun fact—if you were a developing fetus right now, your sensory systems would be so advanced that you could hear voices and even respond to sounds. Which means, spiritually speaking, it's time to start tuning in to what God is saying and responding accordingly!

So, we have witnessed Israel's experience pieced in segments of turmoil and peace. Would you believe that after Deborah's display of courage, Israel slid back into their old habits of evil and found themselves in a seven-year period of Midianite oppression? Some things never change!

But just when Israel thought all hope was lost, God raised up an unlikely hero—Gideon. And guess what? His leadership secured…you guessed it! Another 40 years of peace. Isn't it fascinating that after a four-hundred-year protracted period of slavery and a forty-year wilderness sojourn, God rewards His people in parcels of forties? Let's analyze the details of this new forty-fortune and extract the lessons.

> *"Thus Midian was subdued before the children of Israel, so that they lifted their heads no more. And the country was quiet for forty years in the days of Gideon."*
> ***(Judges 8:28)***

Gideon's story is one of hesitation turned into boldness. When God called him to lead, Gideon was not exactly the picture of confidence. In fact, he was hiding in a winepress, trying to thresh wheat in secret, hoping the Midianites wouldn't notice. And yet, the angel of the Lord greeted him with, "The Lord is with you, mighty warrior!" (Judges 6:12). Talk about an ironic introduction! Gideon didn't see himself as a warrior, but God saw who he could become.

After an elaborate process of divine reassurance—including the famous fleece test—Gideon finally embraced his calling. But just as he was getting comfortable with the idea of leading an army, God threw him another curveball. His army of 32,000 men was reduced to just 300. That's not a typo—300 men to face a Midianite army described as thick as locusts. But God was making a point: victory was never about numbers but about faith.

Armed with nothing but trumpets, torches, and jars, Gideon and his 300 men executed a brilliant psychological warfare strategy. In the middle of the night, they surrounded the enemy camp, smashed their jars, blew their trumpets, and shouted, "A sword for the Lord and for Gideon!" (Judges 7:20). The Midianites, in sheer panic, turned on each other and fled. The battle was won before Israel had to lift a sword.

And just like that, Israel experienced 40 years of peace.

This story teaches us that God often calls us to step out in faith even when we feel unqualified. Gideon's journey from fearful to fearless reminds us that God doesn't look for the strongest, the most equipped, or the most confident—He looks for those who are willing.

And since your spiritual ears are fine-tuned at this stage, maybe it's time to stop doubting and start listening. If God could use Gideon, He can certainly use you. So next time He calls, don't be like Gideon in the winepress—be like Gideon with the trumpet!

Reflection:

- Have you ever felt unqualified for something God has called you to do? How did you respond?
- How can you rely on God's strength instead of your own abilities?

- Are there any fears or insecurities holding you back from stepping into what God has for you?

Gideon started out hiding, afraid, and unsure of himself. But by trusting God, he stepped into his mighty warrior identity and led Israel into 40 years of peace. Your fears don't define you—God's call does. What battle are you facing today that requires you to step forward in faith?

Affirmation:

I am not defined by my fears but by God's calling. I choose faith over hesitation and obedience over doubt. Like Gideon, I will step forward with courage, trusting that God's strength is made perfect in my weakness. I am a mighty warrior in His hands, and my obedience will lead to victory and peace.

DAY 20

Quality vs. Quantity – What Truly Matters?

Welcome to Day 20! You've made it to another milestone—just like a growing baby at 20 weeks, you're at the halfway mark! At this stage, movement is strong, reflexes are sharp, and the senses are actively engaging with the world. This is where things get real—where spiritual development moves beyond just forming and starts functioning. Likewise, today's lesson pushes us to examine whether we are truly growing in the right areas or just accumulating for the sake of it.

We've been on quite the forty-filled adventure so far, haven't we? As we dig through these biblical references, one thing keeps popping up: humanity's epic cycle of stumbling and redemption. No matter how many chances God gives, people always seem to find a way to trip over their own feet. But here's the good news—we don't have to repeat their mistakes! These stories aren't just ancient history; they're flashing holographic displays guiding us toward a fortified life in Christ.

Let's take a quick recap tour: We've journeyed from Noah to Isaac, Jacob, and Esau, then onto Moses and the wandering Israelites. We leaped into the era of the Judges, witnessing Othniel, Deborah, and Gideon ushering in forty-year cycles of peace. Now, let's shine the spotlight on a lesser-known judge who came about 68 years after Gideon's rule. His story doesn't come with jaw-dropping battles or legendary victories, but it holds a hidden gem of wisdom wrapped in yet another forty moment. And as we've learned—with God, no number is meaningless!

> *"He had forty sons and thirty grandsons, who rode on seventy donkeys. He judged Israel eight years."*
> ***(Judges 12:14)***

Enter Abdon—a man of impressive numbers. Forty sons. Thirty grandsons. Seventy donkeys. By earthly standards, this guy was thriving! Large family? Check. Visible wealth? Check. Leadership role? Check. But here's the twist—his legacy barely made a dent in Israel's history.

Unlike the great judges before him, Abdon didn't lead groundbreaking victories or spiritual revolutions. His name is mentioned, his stats are recorded, and then...nothing. No inspiring speeches. No nation-shifting reforms. Just a long list of numbers and a leadership period that came and went.

So here's the real question: Are we chasing numbers, or are we chasing meaning?

In today's world, success is often measured by how much we accumulate—more money, more followers, more possessions, more achievements. We're constantly being told that bigger is better. More means you've made it. But Abdon's story whispers a different truth: Quantity without impact is just noise.

You can have thousands of followers but leave no lasting influence. You can have a massive family but fail to nurture deep spiritual roots. You can hold a position of power but make no meaningful difference.

God isn't impressed by numbers—He's impressed by faithfulness. He values people who invest in what truly matters: transformed lives, genuine relationships, and eternal impact. So, let's call this "the forty-donkey syndrome"—the illusion that status, wealth, and outward success equal significance when, in reality, only what's done for Christ will last.

Reflection:

- Am I pursuing success in quantity or faithfulness in quality?
- What am I building that will last beyond my lifetime?
- How can I shift my focus from earthly status to eternal significance?
- Do I suffer from "the forty-donkey syndrome," valuing status over spiritual impact?

Abdon had many sons and great wealth, but his spiritual impact was forgotten. We have the opportunity to build something greater—a life that glorifies God and leaves a lasting imprint. Will you spend your days chasing things that fade, or will you commit to what truly matters? What legacy will you start building today?

Affirmation:

I choose to build a life of eternal significance. My worth is not measured by numbers, but by faithfulness to God's purpose. I reject the illusion of success without impact and commit to investing in what truly matters. I will leave a legacy of faith, love, and purpose that honors God and transforms lives.

DAY 21

CREEPING COMPROMISE

Welcome to Day 21! You've made it this far—properly purged, spiritually alert, and hopefully not too traumatized by Israel's habit of running back into trouble like a toddler drawn to an uncovered electrical outlet. Seriously, after everything they had been through, you'd think they'd finally learn! But alas, history repeats itself.

We're still deep in the era of judges, and by now, Israel's faithfulness is as fleeting as a social media trend. One minute they're singing victory songs, and the next, they're willingly handing the aux cord to their oppressors. Even with clear evidence that obedience brings blessing and rebellion leads to disaster, they kept toeing the line between loyalty and waywardness—only to face the consequences yet again.

There is no direct biblical evidence that Abdon contributed to the Philistine conquest or downfall. However, insights from Judges 12:13-15 suggest that his tenure, though peaceful, was unremarkable. No great military victories, no recorded spiritual reforms—just a focus on wealth and family. His leadership, marked by possible complacency, was followed by forty years of Philistine oppression after his death. Translation? The cycle of compromise continued, and Israel once again found itself shackled—both physically and spiritually.

> *"And the children of Israel did evil again in the sight of the Lord; and the Lord delivered them into the hand of the Philistines forty years."*
> ***(Judges 13:1)***

For forty years, Israel suffered under Philistine rule, trapped in an exhausting loop of disobedience and divine discipline. But even in their darkest moments, God was already laying the groundwork for deliverance. That plan came in the form of Samson—a man literally set apart from birth with supernatural strength and a divine calling.

Samson's story began with a miraculous birth announcement. His mother, previously barren, received a visit from an angel who gave her specific instructions: Samson was to be a Nazirite from the womb—no wine, no unclean food, and no haircuts. His very existence was a reminder that God was still at work among His people. He was chosen to begin Israel's deliverance, but his life would become a cautionary tale about how small compromises lead to colossal consequences.

Though Samson had the physical power of a Marvel superhero, his spiritual strength was another story. He was driven by impulse, pursuing relationships outside of God's will, making reckless choices, and relying more on his gift than the Giver. His greatest downfall, however, was his inability to recognize the slow erosion of his calling. Each compromise seemed harmless—until it wasn't.

Then came Delilah, a woman whose influence over Samson would prove to be his greatest test—the Philistine femme fatale who made betrayal look like a romantic subplot. Samson, blinded by desire and overestimating his invincibility, ignored every red flag. Delilah persistently pressured him to reveal the source of his strength, and though he resisted at first, his guard slowly lowered. What began as a game of deception turned into a devastating downfall. When he finally disclosed his secret, he didn't realize that his strength had left him—until it was too late.

The mighty warrior became a blind prisoner, reduced to grinding grain in the house of his enemies. The same Philistines he was born to defeat were now his captors, mocking him in humiliation. This is the insidious nature of compromise—it rarely demands an immediate price. Instead, it creeps in subtly, disguising itself as harmless, until one day, we wake up and realize we are no longer who we were meant to be.

Yet, even in failure, Samson's story didn't end in defeat. In his final moment, he turned back to God, praying for strength one last time. With renewed faith, he brought down the temple of the Philistines, striking a final blow against Israel's oppressors. Though he had stumbled, God still used him in the end.

Much like a developing child at twenty-one weeks, where senses are heightened and responses to external stimuli become more pronounced, we must become more aware of the subtle dangers of compromise. Just as a baby starts to react more intentionally to sound and movement, we need to train our spiritual reflexes to respond to warning signs before we drift too far. The question is, are we paying attention, or are we playing with fire and hoping not to get burned?

Reflection:

- Am I allowing small compromises to weaken my spiritual walk?
- Have I placed more trust in my gifts than in my relationship with God?
- Are there warning signs in my life that I am ignoring?
- What steps can I take to resist temptation and stay fully committed to God's calling?

Samson was chosen, empowered, and set apart, but his gradual compromises led to his downfall. The enemy is patient—he doesn't need you to fall overnight. He just needs you to take one small step in the wrong direction, again and again. May Samson's story serve as both a warning and a challenge—stand firm in faith, guard against creeping compromise, and use your God-given strength for His purpose rather than allowing the enemy to steal your calling.

Affirmation:

I will remain steadfast in my faith, refusing to compromise my calling. I choose obedience over convenience, discipline over impulse, and faith over fleeting desires. I will not allow subtle distractions to weaken my spiritual foundation. My strength is in God, and I will walk in His purpose with clarity, conviction, and unwavering commitment.

DAY 22

Breaking Under the Burden of Bias

Welcome to Day 22! At twenty-two weeks, a growing child's brain is undergoing rapid development, forming countless neural connections that shape their ability to think, feel, and respond. Their sense of touch is refining, allowing them to explore their surroundings in the womb, responding to stimuli in ways that indicate awareness and sensitivity. Their ability to hear, react, and even recognize voices is increasing. They are no longer just growing—they are responding. And just like in spiritual growth, the more we develop, the more accountable we become for what we hear and how we respond. Today, we look at a judge who heard but failed to act—Eli.

We've been in the era of the Judges for a while now, and today, we introduce our final judge. But before we dive in, let's pause for some forty-club trivia. Othniel, Deborah, and Gideon all secured forty years of peace for Israel. That's three consecutive cycles of forty! And then there was Ehud—oh, how could we forget him? He didn't just match them; he doubled their record, securing eighty years of peace! Let's take a moment to applaud Ehud for his remarkable contribution. If you haven't studied him yet, now's the perfect time to do some Bible detective work and share what you find.

Now, let's talk about someone who didn't quite make the hall of fame in the same way. Samson, the strongest man to ever live, only judged for twenty years. Could it be that his tenure was cut short because of compromise? That's something to think about. But today, our focus shifts to another forty-year judge—one who carried both political and spiritual authority but ultimately failed in his role. Eli, the priest and judge whose tenure ended in tragedy.

> *"And it came to pass, when he made mention of the ark of God, that he fell from off the seat backward by the side of the gate, and his neck broke, and he died: for he was an old man, and heavy. And he had judged Israel forty years."*
> ***(1 Samuel 4:18)***

Eli had great potential. For forty years, he guided Israel as both high priest and judge, making him the only man to hold both offices simultaneously. He had the privilege of mentoring Samuel, the future prophet of Israel. Yet, despite his esteemed position, Eli's legacy is one of failure, not because he was a wicked man, but because he failed to confront wrongdoing—especially within his own household.

Eli's sons, Hophni and Phinehas, were notorious for their corruption. They abused their priestly roles, disrespected God's sacrifices, and shamelessly led Israel into sin. The people recognized their wickedness, and more importantly, God saw it too. But how did Eli, their father, respond? A weak rebuke—nothing more. He chose personal attachment over accountability.

And here's where it gets dangerous. Personal bias can cloud our judgment. When we allow favoritism, fear, or personal ties to override our duty to stand for truth, we set ourselves up for failure. Eli's refusal to take a firm stand cost him everything. His sons were killed in battle, the Ark of the Covenant was captured, and upon hearing the news, Eli himself fell backward, broke his neck, and died.

Eli's story is a sobering reminder that turning a blind eye to sin only leads to disaster. He wasn't ignorant—he chose not to act. His passivity and bias led to the downfall of his household and Israel's greatest spiritual loss at that time. Excusing sin because of personal ties doesn't protect anyone; it only fuels corruption until it consumes everything in its path.

Just as a child in the womb experiences rapid brain growth and heightened sensitivity to touch, becoming more aware of its environment, we too must learn to respond correctly to God's voice. Eli heard God's warnings but did not respond. Will we make the same mistake, or will we act when God calls us to confront and correct what is wrong?

Reflection:

- Are there areas in my life where I excuse sin or wrongdoing because of personal bias?
- Do I avoid confrontation to maintain comfort, even when truth is at stake?
- How can I be more intentional in standing for truth without fear or favoritism?

Eli's story teaches us that leadership without accountability leads to ruin. When we fail to confront sin, we don't just damage ourselves—we harm everyone around us. Let's choose integrity over complacency and stand firm in God's truth, even when it's difficult.

Affirmation:

I choose to stand for truth, even when it is uncomfortable. I will not let personal bias cloud my judgment or prevent me from confronting what is wrong. I walk in integrity, accountability, and obedience to God's call. My leadership, influence, and decisions will reflect His righteousness, and I will not turn a blind eye to what He has revealed to me.

DAY 23

THE WEIGHT OF A CROWN OF PRIDE AND JEALOUSY

Welcome to Day 23! Whoo! We have completed the judges, and now it's time to step into the era of the kings. Do you see the divine pattern unfolding? We started with Noah, the prophet, then journeyed through the patriarchs (Isaac, Jacob) and Brother Esau, returned to a prophet (Moses), transitioned to the judges—including Deborah, a prophetess, and Eli, a priest—and now we arrive at the kings. Each shift has brought deeper lessons, and this next phase is no different. Where will this lead? Stay fortified, and you will see!

Yesterday, we reflected on Eli's failure to act, how his inability to confront wrongdoing led to his downfall, and how our own reluctance to address sin can have serious consequences. As we move forward, we see Israel shifting once again—this time, from spiritual leaders to earthly rulers. The people desired a king, despite God's warnings, revealing their ongoing struggle to trust in divine leadership.

Israel begged for a king, determined to be like the other nations. God warned them of the consequences, but they insisted. Sound familiar? Just as their ancestors stubbornly resisted God's plan approximately 400 years prior in the wilderness for forty years, their descendants still carried the same spirit of impatience and self-reliance. What would this new decision bring?

> *"And afterward they desired a king: and God gave unto them Saul the son of Cis, a man of the tribe of Benjamin, by the space of forty years."*
> ***(Acts 13:21)***

For forty years, Saul sat on Israel's throne—a reign that began with divine appointment but ended in self-destruction. The people had demanded a king, despite God's warnings, and in response, He gave them Saul. At first, Saul showed great promise, displaying humility and strength. But as time passed, the very qualities that made him a strong leader were overshadowed by pride, insecurity, and jealousy. Instead of humbling himself before God, Saul let his emotions take control, and in doing so, he distanced himself from God's will.

Saul's jealousy of David became his undoing. Rather than embracing his role and trusting in God's sovereignty, he became consumed by the fear that someone else would take his place. His obsession led him to make rash decisions, directly disobey God's commands, and isolate himself from those who could have guided him back to obedience. His story serves as a stark reminder that unchecked jealousy and pride can blind us to the very blessings God has given us, leading us to make choices that pull us further from His presence.

Saul's reign did not just affect him—it affected the entire nation. His failures led to instability, spiritual decline, and a fractured kingdom. His disobedience caused suffering among his people, proving that a leader's spiritual health directly impacts those they lead. Israel, once so eager for a human king, was forced to realize that no ruler could replace God's perfect leadership.

This teaches us that our personal choices do not just affect us; they influence those around us—our families, workplaces, ministries, and even future generations. Saul's story challenges us to evaluate whether we are leading our own lives in a way that honors God or if we are allowing pride and fear to dictate our actions. Are we making choices that strengthen our faith and the faith of those around us, or are we walking a path that leads to unnecessary struggles?

Reflection:

- Am I allowing jealousy, pride, or insecurity to shape my decisions and relationships?
- How can I guard my heart against these emotions and trust God's plan for my life?
- How can I cultivate humility and obedience so that my legacy reflects God's purpose rather than personal ambition?
- How are my personal choices influencing those around me—am I leading others closer to God or further away?

Saul's forty-year reign was not ended by external enemies, but by the internal battles he failed to surrender to God. His life is a warning that leadership, influence, and even divine calling mean little if not accompanied by humility and trust in God. His failures impacted not just himself but an entire nation, proving that personal disobedience often has communal consequences. As you seek to fortify your life, remember that unchecked pride and jealousy are like weeds that choke the life out of God's blessings. But through self-awareness, surrender, and trust in Him, we can detox our hearts and cultivate a spirit of humility and contentment. Are you ready to let go and trust God's plan?

Affirmation:

I reject jealousy, pride, and fear, choosing instead to walk in humility and trust in God's plan. My worth is not threatened by the success of others, for I am secure in my divine purpose. I will lead my life with integrity, ensuring that my choices bring glory to God and uplift those around me. My heart is surrendered, my motives are pure, and my steps are guided by His wisdom.

DAY 24

"THE GIANT SLAYER'S MINDSET"

Welcome to Day 24! Yesterday, we tackled the dangers of pride and jealousy and embraced the power of humility and contentment. But today? Today, we pick up our slingshots—because it's time to slay some giants!

At twenty-four weeks, a developing child's lungs are maturing, preparing for the breath of life, while their brain is refining the ability to process signals and respond to external stimuli. They're not just growing—they're gearing up to make their grand entrance. Likewise, today's lesson reminds us that our spiritual lungs must be filled with faith, and our spiritual reflexes must be trained to react to challenges with trust in God. Because, let's be honest, we've all had a Goliath standing in our way at some point, and cowering in fear isn't and has never been the best battle plan.

David was anointed as king while Saul was still reigning. Saul had lost the Spirit of the Lord, and David was anointed in secret. From that day, the Spirit of the Lord came powerfully upon David (1 Samuel 16:13). Though the world didn't yet recognize him as king, he was already chosen and equipped by God. So, while Goliath taunted the Israelite army, strutting around like he was the undisputed champion of intimidation, he had no idea that a teenage shepherd with a slingshot and an unshakable faith was about to humble him—on the 40th day.

> *"And the Philistine drew near morning and evening, and presented himself forty days."*
> ***(1 Samuel 17:16)***

For forty days, Goliath stood before Israel, flexing his muscles, hurling insults, and daring anyone to step forward. Morning and evening, his voice thundered through the valley, paralyzing even the strongest warriors. The Israelites were stuck in a fear loop, replaying the worst-case scenario in their minds. No one dared to move.

Then came David—a shepherd boy, overlooked by everyone except God. While trained soldiers saw an unbeatable giant, David saw an uncircumcised Philistine flapping his gum endlessly, delivering an unsolicited masterclass in arrogance. He understood that Goliath's size didn't matter because the God who had delivered him before would do it again. So, with one stone, one slingshot, and one unshakable belief, David took down the giant that had terrorized Israel for forty days.

Just like a developing child's lungs prepare for life outside the womb, our faith must be strengthened before the battle comes. We don't wait until we face giants to start building trust in God—we train daily, breathing in His promises so that when fear tries to suffocate us, faith becomes our natural response. If a baby can prep for the real world without even realizing it, we can certainly prepare our faith for the battles ahead!

This story is more than a legendary battle; it is a giant-slaying guidebook. Fear, doubt, insecurity, addiction, financial struggles, broken relationships—these giants stand before us, taunting and paralyzing us, making us believe that victory is impossible. But David's victory reminds us that no enemy, no obstacle, no giant is greater than the God who fights for us. The key is not in our own strength but in our willingness to step forward in faith, believing that God is bigger than whatever we face.

So, what's your giant? And more importantly, are you ready to take your shot?

Reflection:

- What giants have been standing in my way, keeping me stuck in fear or discouragement?

- Am I looking at my challenges through the lens of fear or through the lens of faith?
- How can I shift my mindset to trust that God is bigger than my biggest battle?

Goliath taunted Israel for forty days, but it only took one moment of faith to bring him down. The longer we allow our giants to intimidate us, the more power they seem to have. But the truth is, they fall the moment we step forward with the mindset of a giant slayer—one who trusts not in their own strength, but in the unstoppable power of God. Will you face your giant today?

Affirmation:

I am a giant slayer! I do not shrink back in fear, for my faith is greater than any obstacle before me. I choose to see my battles through the lens of victory, knowing that God has already equipped me for triumph. No enemy, no doubt, no fear can stand against the power of my God. I will step forward with boldness, knowing that every giant must fall in the presence of His mighty hand.

DAY 25

THE DANGER OF FALSE CROWNS

Welcome to Day 25! You are doing an incredible job on this journey. Now that you have embraced "the giant slayer mindset," it's time for some introspection. Yesterday, we witnessed how David stepped boldly into his calling, taking down Goliath with a single stone. But today, we examine what happens when someone steps into a role that was never theirs to fill. Because while some are busy slaying giants, others are busy wearing crowns that don't belong to them—and that, my friends, is a recipe for disaster.

At twenty-five weeks, a developing child's brain is rapidly growing, fine-tuning motor skills and responses. The movements are more deliberate, purposeful, and controlled. Spiritually, this stage reminds us that we, too, must become more intentional about our choices. Not every throne is meant for us, and not every crown is ours to wear.

God has called us to be a royal priesthood, but not all authority is God-given. There are positions we should not aspire to and roles we were never meant to fill. Just because an opportunity is available doesn't mean it aligns with God's plan for us. It's easy to be swayed by expectations, ambition, or even fear of missing out, but stepping outside of God's will can lead to unnecessary struggles.

Let's talk about a king who seized a throne that was never his to claim—someone who, like Lucifer, coveted a position that was not his for the taking. Interestingly, like Esau, he reached the age of forty, a pivotal time often associated with transition and testing in the Bible. But unlike Moses or David, he was not divinely called to his position—he was merely a placeholder.

> *"Ishbosheth, Saul's son, was forty years old when he became king over Israel, and he reigned two years."* ***(2 Samuel 2:10)***

Ishbosheth's reign began at forty, a number symbolizing testing and transition. While others used this season as a steppingstone to greatness, Ishbosheth found himself in a position he was never equipped to hold. He was not God's chosen king. Instead, he was a desperate attempt to prolong Saul's legacy—a man-made king ruling on borrowed time.

God had already anointed David as Israel's rightful king. Yet, in an effort to resist this divine transition, Abner, Saul's military commander, installed Ishbosheth as king. This was not an act of obedience, but of human intervention—a refusal to accept God's new direction.

Without God's anointing, Ishbosheth's reign lacked authority, stability, and strength. He ruled in title alone, not by divine calling, relying on others to keep him in power. He was a king without conviction, courage, or the backing of God. When Abner, his strongest ally, defected to David's side, Ishbosheth was left exposed and vulnerable. Shortly after, he was assassinated, and his fragile rule crumbled.

Ishbosheth's story serves as a powerful warning: positions, titles, and influence mean nothing without God's calling. Just because an opportunity presents itself does not mean it is from God. We must discern whether we are stepping into something by His direction or by human ambition.

This applies directly to our everyday decisions—our careers, relationships, ministries, and personal pursuits. Are we making choices out of pressure, insecurity, or the expectations of others? Or are we walking in God's purpose and timing? Pursuing something outside of God's will often leads to stress, instability, and exhaustion because we are trying to sustain something He never ordained. But when we step into God's appointed plan, we move with grace, strength, and divine backing.

Like a child in the womb preparing for life beyond, we must allow God to develop us before stepping into positions that require more than we are ready to handle. Because unlike Ishbosheth, we don't want to wear crowns that were never fitted for our heads.

Reflection:

- Am I pursuing something because God has called me to it, or because others expect it of me?
- Have I taken the time to seek God's confirmation before stepping into leadership, relationships, or major life decisions?
- Am I struggling to maintain something that God never assigned to me?
- How can I trust God's timing rather than forcing opportunities that He has not anointed?

Ishbosheth had the title of king, but he never had the anointing. His reign was marked by fear and instability because he was never God's choice. We must be careful not to step into places that God has not called us to occupy. Instead, we should wait on His anointing, knowing that what He appoints, He sustains.

Are you chasing a crown that God never placed on your head, or are you waiting for His divine direction?

Affirmation:

I trust God's divine timing for my life. I will not chase positions, titles, or opportunities that He has not assigned to me. I reject the pressure to meet human expectations and instead wait for the anointing that comes from Him alone. What God ordains, He sustains, and I walk boldly in His purpose, confident that His plan is always better than mine.

DAY 26

"THE CHASE: RUNNING AFTER GOD'S HEART"

Welcome to Day 26! Yesterday, we talked about false crowns—grabbing for titles, positions, and recognition that God never intended for us. But today, we shift gears. No more chasing after empty status—it's time to chase after something of true substance and lasting significance. Forget the throne, the crown, and the applause. Today, we're going after what truly matters: God's heart.

If yesterday was about wearing the wrong crown, today is about pursuing the right King. David wasn't perfect, but one thing set him apart—he was relentless in his desire to know and please God. He faltered greatly, yet he always found his way back to God. That's the kind of chase we're after—running full speed, not after power, success, or approval, but after the very heart of God.

> *"And the days that David reigned over Israel were forty years: seven years reigned he in Hebron, and thirty and three years reigned he in Jerusalem."*
> ***(1 Kings 2:11)***

For forty years, David sat on Israel's throne—not as a man without fault, but as a man who refused to let his failures define him. His leadership was forged through trials, victories, and heartbreaking mistakes, but through it all, he never stopped seeking God. This wasn't just about ruling a nation; it was about maintaining a relationship with the One who had placed him there.

David's journey was anything but smooth. Before he wore the crown, he spent years running for his life, hunted by King Saul. Even when he became king, his struggles didn't end. He fell into sin—adultery with Bathsheba, devising a murder, and failing to correct his own household's dysfunction. Yet, what distinguished David from Saul was not his perfection, but his response to conviction. When the prophet Nathan confronted him, he didn't justify, blame, or cover up his sin—he repented. His psalms are filled with raw, unfiltered cries to God, showing a heart that knew true restoration could only come from Him.

Despite his flaws, David pursued God in ways that changed Israel's history. He brought back the Ark of the Covenant, reestablished worship in Jerusalem, and sought to build a temple for God. Though he wasn't allowed to complete the temple, he didn't respond with disappointment or entitlement—he spent his final years preparing the way for Solomon to do what he could not. David understood that chasing after God wasn't just about personal success, but about leaving a lasting impact that would point future generations toward Him.

David's forty-year reign is proof that pursuing God's heart doesn't mean living without failure—it means refusing to stay in failure. It means prioritizing His presence over personal ambition, His will over our own, and His legacy over temporary achievements. A heart that chases after God isn't concerned with looking perfect—it's concerned with staying close.

Much like a developing child whose heart is growing stronger, pumping life through the body and sustaining every function, our spiritual hearts must be strengthened through the pursuit of God. Just as a fetus depends on the steady rhythm of its heartbeat for survival, we must rely on God's heartbeat to sustain our spiritual lives. Running after Him isn't about speed; it's about consistency, connection, and dependence. So, the question is: Is your heart beating in sync with His?

Reflection:

- When I fail, do I hide from God or run toward Him in repentance?
- How am I actively seeking God's heart in my daily decisions, priorities, and worship?
- Am I building a legacy that reflects my own desires, or one that prepares the next generation to know and follow God?

David's life teaches us that God isn't looking for perfect people—He's looking for pursuers. His forty-year reign was not built on flawless choices, but on a relentless commitment to return to God, again and again. Success in God's kingdom isn't measured by how few mistakes we make, but by how quickly we turn back when we fall. So today, let's drop the pursuit of status, perfection, and recognition, and chase after the only thing that truly matters—God's heart.

Affirmation:

I am a pursuer of God's heart. My failures do not define me—my response to them does. I will seek His presence above all else, knowing that in Him, I find true fulfillment. I choose to run after His will, His ways, and His wisdom, making my life a reflection of His grace and truth. My heart beats in sync with His, and I will never stop chasing after Him.

DAY 27

THE MEASURE OF GODLY WISDOM

Welcome to Day 27! So, Saul ruled for forty years, David did his forty, and now it's Solomon's turn to run the forty-year marathon. But before we roll out the red carpet for Israel's golden age, let's take a moment to appreciate the weight of the crown. Leadership isn't just about looking regal and waving at the crowds—it's about how you rule when no one's watching. Yesterday, we explored the importance of pursuing God's heart. Today, we examine the wisdom needed to stay aligned with Him when the blessings flow.

At twenty-seven weeks, the mother's body is adapting to the growing weight of the baby. Her lungs work harder to provide oxygen, and her center of gravity shifts, requiring her to maintain balance and endurance. Meanwhile, the baby is more active than ever—stretching, kicking, and responding to external stimuli. This constant movement reminds the mother that she is carrying something with great purpose, something that will soon enter a new stage of life. Much like this process, wisdom isn't just about gaining knowledge, it's about preparing for the responsibilities that come with it. The transition from carrying a child to giving birth requires strength, endurance, and careful preparation. Similarly, stepping into leadership or a position of influence, as Solomon did, demands readiness, maturity, and a firm foundation in wisdom. Just as a mother adjusts to the reality of nurturing life, we must learn to adjust to the weight of wisdom, ensuring that we respond to challenges with discernment and maturity.

Let's talk about how Solomon acquired and adjusted to the weight of wisdom. Imagine being handed the keys to an entire kingdom with one wish—anything you desire. Riches? Power? Victory over your enemies? Most rulers wouldn't think twice. But Solomon's request was different. When given the chance to ask for anything, he didn't choose wealth or military dominance. He asked for wisdom. That one decision set the tone for a reign unlike any other.

> *"And the time that Solomon reigned in Jerusalem over all Israel was forty years."*
> ***(1 Kings 11:42)***

For forty years, King Solomon ruled over Israel, a reign that began with immense promise. Pleased with his request, God granted him unparalleled wisdom, along with riches and honor beyond what any king before or after him would possess. His name became synonymous with divine wisdom, and his reign ushered in an era of peace and prosperity unlike any Israel had known.

Under Solomon's leadership, Israel flourished. He built the magnificent temple in Jerusalem, fulfilling the dream his father David had prepared for. Leaders from distant nations traveled to witness his wisdom firsthand, seeking counsel from the king whose understanding was unmatched. His proverbs and writings revealed deep insights into life, leadership, and the fear of the Lord as the foundation of true wisdom.

But as the years passed, Solomon drifted from the wisdom he had once sought so earnestly. He compromised his devotion to God, forming alliances with foreign nations through marriage, adopting their customs, and tolerating idolatry in Israel. His once-pure heart, fully devoted to the Lord, became divided. Though he had been blessed with wisdom, he failed to apply it fully to his own life, allowing his desires to overshadow his discernment.

Solomon's reign teaches us that godly wisdom is not just about possessing knowledge but about applying it faithfully throughout our lives. Wisdom without obedience leads to compromise, and compromise leads to downfall. Just as a mother's body strengthens in preparation for childbirth, we must strengthen our spiritual discipline so that our responses to life's challenges reflect God's truth. We can be gifted with intelligence, discernment, and understanding, but if we do not stay rooted in God's wisdom, we risk being led astray by our own desires.

And let's be real—what's the point of having all the wisdom in the world if we ignore it when it matters most? Solomon started as the wisest man alive, but by the end of his forty-year reign, he looked more like a cautionary tale than a role model. So, the question is: will we just accumulate knowledge, or will we actually apply it?

Reflection:

- Am I actively seeking godly wisdom, not just for knowledge, but for daily application?
- Are there areas in my life where I know the right thing to do but struggle to follow through in obedience?
- How can I guard my heart against compromise and ensure that my pursuit of wisdom aligns with my pursuit of God?

Solomon's reign reminds us that wisdom is a gift, but its true power lies in how we use it. His forty years as king were marked by both brilliance and failure, showing us that even the wisest among us are vulnerable when they drift from God. May we not only seek wisdom but also the discipline to walk in it daily, ensuring that our pursuit of knowledge never replaces our devotion to the One who gives it.

Affirmation:

I seek godly wisdom, not just for knowledge, but for transformation. I will apply what God teaches me, guarding my heart against compromise and walking in obedience. My wisdom will be rooted in truth, my leadership will reflect His guidance, and my decisions will honor Him. I choose wisdom that sustains, wisdom that builds, and wisdom that glorifies the One who gives it.

DAY 28

THE POWER OF A WHISPER

Welcome to Day 28! After exploring all these kings and assessing their strengths and weaknesses, do you feel ready for royal responsibilities? Remember, we are royal in God's sight.

The reign of the kings is not over just yet! But before we continue their saga, let's pause for a royal intermission and meet a prophet who had one of the grandest forty encounters in history. But for context, let's connect the dots. After Solomon's reign, the kingdom was split in two: the Northern Kingdom of Israel and the Southern Kingdom of Judah. Fifty years after Solomon's reign, Ahab became the seventh king of the Northern Kingdom. He was wicked. God raised up His prophet Elijah to warn him. After the fire showdown on Mount Carmel, Elijah had to run for his life in fear of Jezebel. He ran to Horeb.

> *"So he arose, and ate and drank; and he went in the strength of that food forty days and forty nights as far as Horeb, the mountain of God."*
> ***(1 Kings 19:8)***

For forty days and forty nights, Elijah journeyed to Mount Horeb, the mountain of God. He had just experienced a dramatic victory on Mount Carmel, calling down fire from heaven and proving before Israel that the Lord alone is God. Yet, in the wake of this triumph, fear overtook him. Queen Jezebel sought his life, and Elijah, weary and discouraged, fled into the wilderness.

At his lowest point, Elijah collapsed beneath a broom tree and prayed that he might die. But instead of rebuke, God responded with provision. An angel touched him, offering food and water, sustaining him for the long journey ahead. Strengthened by this divine nourishment, Elijah pressed on until he reached Horeb, where he encountered God in an unexpected way.

At the mountain, Elijah witnessed a mighty wind, a violent earthquake, and a consuming fire. But God was not in these grand displays. Then came a gentle whisper—a still, small voice. In that quiet moment, Elijah experienced the presence of God in a way that no miracle or spectacle had provided.

This moment reminds us of something truly remarkable. At 28 weeks, a developing baby can now recognize their mother's voice, responding to familiar sounds in the womb. The noise of the world might be loud, but the baby learns to tune in to the one voice that provides comfort, security, and love. Similarly, Elijah had to silence the noise of fear, discouragement, and external chaos to hear God's gentle whisper.

Elijah's journey teaches us that spiritual renewal does not always come through dramatic interventions but in the quiet places where we lean in to hear God's voice. Just as a baby instinctively recognizes the voice of the one who carries them, we must attune our hearts to recognize God's whisper amid life's storms. When trials leave us drained and disheartened, God does not leave us to fend for ourselves. He provides strength for the journey, not always in the way we expect, but always in the way we need.

Reflection:

- Am I seeking God only in grand, miraculous moments, or am I making space to hear His still, small voice?
- How has God sustained me in seasons of exhaustion and discouragement?
- What steps can I take to quiet my heart and listen for God's guidance?

Elijah's forty-day journey reminds us that God is present, even in our weakest moments. His provision is sufficient, His strength sustains, and His voice still speaks—not in the chaos, but in the stillness. May we learn to trust in His presence, even when the journey is long, and find renewal in the quiet whisper of His love.

Affirmation:

I choose to quiet my heart and listen for God's voice. I will not be distracted by the noise of the world but will lean into the stillness where His presence dwells. Even in exhaustion and uncertainty, I trust in His provision, knowing He sustains me for the journey ahead. His whisper is enough, and I find strength, peace, and renewal in His presence.

DAY 29

THE DANGER OF DEPENDENCE

Welcome to Day 29! You are well on your path of fortification, and heaven is cheering you on. By now, your spiritual discernment should be sharpening, helping you recognize God's voice and stand firm in faith. But let's be real—having a great start doesn't always guarantee a strong finish. That's why today, we're talking about a king who wore the crown but lacked the conviction—a leader whose faith was on spiritual life support, dependent on someone else. And when that person was gone, so was his devotion.

Now, let's talk about the youngest king to ever rule Judah. Picture this: a seven-year-old with a crown on his head, a scepter in his hand, and possibly still struggling with his multiplication tables. That's Joash. He was barely old enough to tie his sandals, yet he was entrusted with a kingdom. Sound like a disaster waiting to happen? Surprisingly, it wasn't—at least, not at first.

> *"Joash was seven years old when he became king, and he reigned forty years in Jerusalem."*
> ***(2 Chronicles 24:1)***

Here's where things take an interesting turn. Joash's story began in secrecy and survival. His entire family was wiped out by the wicked Queen Athaliah, who was determined to exterminate the royal line. But God had other plans. Rescued by his aunt Jehosheba, Joash was hidden in the temple for six years—talk about an unconventional childhood. Instead of growing up in a palace, he was raised in the house of God, under the guidance of the faithful priest Jehoiada.

With Jehoiada as his mentor, Joash flourished. He led efforts to restore the temple, reestablish worship, and bring Israel back to God. The nation thrived under his leadership, and for years, he did what was right in the sight of the Lord. His reign held the promise of renewal and faithfulness.

But here's the problem—Joash's devotion wasn't truly his own. It was borrowed faith, propped up by Jehoiada's wisdom and influence. As long as the priest was alive, Joash stayed on the right path. But when Jehoiada died, the thin veneer of his faith cracked, and everything unraveled.

Without his godly mentor, Joash became a spiritual tumbleweed, blown in whatever direction the wind of influence took him. He surrounded himself with new advisors—men who had no regard for God. Under their persuasion, he abandoned the temple he once restored and embraced idolatry. When God sent prophets to warn him, he refused to listen. And in a moment of chilling irony, Joash ordered the death of Zechariah, Jehoiada's own son, repaying his mentor's legacy with bloodshed.

The king, who had once been a beacon of restoration, became a cautionary tale of rebellion. His downfall was swift. Enemies rose against him, and in a dramatic twist of poetic justice, his own servants betrayed and assassinated him. Joash died not as a celebrated king but as a tragic figure—proof that starting well means nothing if you don't finish well.

Joash's story is a wake-up call. It forces us to ask: Is our faith truly personal, or are we just riding on someone else's? Are we deeply rooted in God, or do we crumble the moment our support system disappears?

It's easy to stay on the right path when we're surrounded by godly mentors, encouraging friends, and a strong spiritual community. But what happens when that changes? What if a spiritual leader we admire falls? What if our environment shifts, and we find ourselves alone in our faith?

Our relationship with God must be personal—not secondhand faith inherited from those around us. Mentors are a blessing, but they are not our foundation—God is.

Otherwise, when the voices around us change, our convictions will waver, and we risk drifting from the truth.

And let's not forget the lesson of influence. Just as wise counsel can uplift us, ungodly influence can destroy us. Joash surrounded himself with corrupt advisors after Jehoiada's death, and it cost him everything. Who are we listening to? Who is shaping our decisions? Are we being guided toward God, or away from Him?

Forty years on the throne should have produced wisdom, strength, and legacy. Instead, Joash's forty years serve as a warning: Spiritual longevity means nothing without spiritual depth.

Reflection:

- Am I building a personal relationship with God, or is my faith dependent on the influence of others?
- Do I surround myself with godly counsel, or do I allow the wrong voices to shape my decisions?
- How do I respond when God convicts me? Am I willing to listen, or do I resist correction?
- What steps am I taking to ensure that I remain faithful to God, not just for a season, but for a lifetime?

Joash's reign teaches us that a good start does not guarantee a strong finish. Faith must be personal, convictions must be guarded, and wise counsel must be chosen carefully. True devotion to God is not measured by temporary obedience but by lifelong faithfulness. May we learn from Joash's mistakes and commit ourselves to finishing well—standing firm in God's truth, no matter what influences surround us.

Affirmation:

My faith is not dependent on the presence of others, but on my personal relationship with God. I will not allow external influences to dictate my devotion. I am deeply rooted in God's truth, discerning in my counsel, and steadfast in my convictions. I will build a faith that endures, ensuring that I finish strong in the purpose God has set before me.

DAY 30

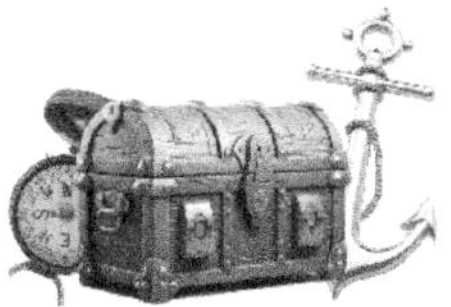

A Call for Change

Welcome to Day 30! Hooray! We have completed the King era. They served us some delectable forty entrées, and now it's time for a spiritual palate cleanser. Imagine God serving a five-course meal—between the heavy dishes of history, He sprinkles in the prophets, refreshing our perspective and redirecting our hearts. Speaking of cleanse, let's talk about a prophet who needed one after running away and finding himself in the belly of a fish. But today, we won't focus on his marine misadventure. Instead, our attention is on his forty-day probationary warning mission.

At thirty weeks, an expectant mother's cravings intensify, and her body demands more nourishment to sustain both herself and the growing life within her. Meanwhile, the baby's appetite is also developing, responding to the nutrients received and preparing for the world outside. Much like the body signals when it's time to refuel, spiritual hunger also sends out warnings. Sometimes, God gives us clear signals that change is needed, yet we push them aside, assuming we have time. Jonah's mission was one such warning—a divine call to spiritual nourishment before it was too late.

> *"Jonah began by going a day's journey into the city, proclaiming, 'Forty more days and Nineveh will be overthrown.'"*
> ***(Jonah 3:4)***

Jonah stood in the heart of Nineveh, his voice echoing through the streets with a message of impending destruction. The city, infamous for its violence and wickedness, had provoked God's judgment, and the decree was clear: in forty days, Nineveh would fall. Yet, woven within this warning was an opportunity—an unspoken invitation to turn from their ways before it was too late.

The people of Nineveh, from the least to the greatest, didn't ignore the warning. Instead, they responded in a way few would have expected. The king himself stripped off his royal robes, clothed himself in sackcloth, and sat in ashes, declaring a citywide fast. Every man, woman, and even the animals were to refrain from eating or drinking as a sign of repentance. They cried out to God, turning from their evil ways, hoping for mercy.

And mercy was given.

God saw their sincerity and relented from the disaster He had planned. The city that had been marked for destruction was spared—not because God changed His mind, but because the people changed their hearts. This wasn't a delayed punishment but a stunning display of divine grace.

Nineveh's story reminds us that God's warnings are not meant to condemn us but to call us back to Him. The forty-day period was not just a countdown to destruction—it was an opportunity for redemption. How often do we ignore God's calls for change, assuming we have more time?

Think about this: Nineveh was a brutal, sinful city, and yet, God gave them a chance. They weren't people who "deserved" grace, yet He extended it anyway. The same is true for us. No matter how far we have drifted, no matter what we've done, God's mercy is still available—but it requires a response.

Too often, we postpone repentance. We tell ourselves, "I'll work on that later," assuming we have all the time in the world. But Nineveh shows us that true transformation happens when we take God's warnings seriously and act immediately. Are there areas in your life where God is calling for change? Will you respond, or will you assume you have time?

Reflection:

- Are there areas in my life where God has been calling me to repentance, but I have ignored Him?
- Do I recognize God's warnings as acts of grace, giving me a chance to turn back before it's too late?
- How can I respond to God's mercy with gratitude and a renewed commitment to righteousness?

The people of Nineveh had forty days to decide their fate, and they chose repentance. God's grace is always available, but it requires a response. If there are areas where you need to turn back to God, don't wait—today is the day of repentance, and His mercy is waiting for you. Will you take the opportunity He has given?

Affirmation:

I choose to respond to God's call for change. I will not delay my repentance or take His grace for granted. Today, I embrace His mercy, turn from anything that separates me from Him, and walk in righteousness. I receive His renewal, knowing that His love is greater than my past. My heart is open, my spirit is willing, and I am transformed by His grace.

DAY 31

THE WEEPING PROPHET'S 40-YEAR WARNING

Welcome to Day 31! You've journeyed through stories of forty-day tests, trials, and triumphs, but today, we meet a prophet whose forty-year mission was marked by something different—tears. If there were an award for the most emotional prophet, Jeremiah would take the gold. Unlike Jonah, who preached and saw a city repent, Jeremiah spent four decades warning Judah, only to be ignored, ridiculed, and attacked. Yesterday, we saw God extend His mercy to a pagan city; today, we see Him repeatedly warn His own people, Judah. But did they listen? Spoiler alert: Not really.

Speaking of tears, did you know that at thirty-one weeks, a mother's hormones are in full swing? It's not unusual for her to cry over a heartfelt commercial, an empty ice cream tub, or simply because her baby decided to practice gymnastics at 2 a.m. Meanwhile, the baby is also developing a strong appetite, swallowing amniotic fluid, and fine-tuning its taste buds. Much like an expectant mother navigating a whirlwind of emotions, Jeremiah carried the emotional weight of a nation that refused to listen—pleading, warning, and weeping for Judah's return to God.

> *"But the Lord said to me, 'Do not say, "I am too young." You must go to everyone I send you to and say whatever I command you. Do not be afraid of them, for I am with you and will rescue you,' declares the Lord."*
> ***(Jeremiah 1:7-8)***

For forty years, Jeremiah faithfully spoke God's words to Judah, warning them to repent before destruction came. Instead of heeding his message, they mocked, imprisoned, and even plotted to kill him. He was thrown into a cistern, labeled a traitor, and left to suffer—yet, he never stopped speaking the truth.

Jeremiah's ministry began during the reign of King Josiah, a time of religious reform. But after Josiah's death, the nation spiraled back into rebellion. They clung to the Temple as their security blanket, believing that because God's house was in Jerusalem, they were untouchable. Jeremiah shattered this illusion, warning that no building or tradition could protect them if their hearts were far from God.

His message was clear: Repent, or face destruction. He prophesied that Babylon would conquer Judah, that Jerusalem would fall, and that exile was imminent. Instead of listening, the people doubled down in their rebellion. They mocked him for prophesying doom, but Jeremiah couldn't keep quiet. Even when he was discouraged, he admitted:

> *"But if I say, 'I will not mention His word or speak anymore in His name,' His word is in my heart like a fire, a fire shut up in my bones. I am weary of holding it in; indeed, I cannot."*
> ***(Jeremiah 20:9)***

Jeremiah's life teaches us that faithfulness to God doesn't always bring immediate rewards or applause. Sometimes, standing firm means standing alone. But here's the twist—while Jeremiah prophesied judgment, he also carried a message of hope:

> *"'For I know the plans I have for you,' declares the Lord, 'plans to prosper you and not to harm you, plans to give you hope and a future.'"*
> ***(Jeremiah 29:11)***

Even in judgment, God's mercy remained. Though exile came, it wasn't the end—God had a plan to restore His people.

Jeremiah's story is a wake-up call. Judah's downfall wasn't sudden, it was the result of repeated warnings ignored. How often do we do the same? God nudges us through His Word, convicts us through the Spirit, and sends people to warn us, yet, we brush it off, thinking we have time. But do we?

Jeremiah also reminds us that obedience isn't always comfortable. We live in a world that often rejects truth, and speaking up for God can come with opposition, ridicule, and even isolation. Are we more concerned with being accepted than being faithful?

And let's not miss the hope in Jeremiah's message. Even when we've messed up, God still has a plan. He is a God of restoration, willing to rebuild what was broken—but we must turn back to Him.

Reflection:

- When have I felt discouraged for standing firm in my faith?
- Am I willing to obey God, even if it means facing resistance and rejection?
- How can I trust that God's plans are still good, even when my circumstances are difficult?

Jeremiah's forty-year ministry was marked by suffering, but he remained faithful. Success in God's eyes isn't measured by popularity—it's measured by obedience. When the world rejects truth, will you still stand firm? Will you remain faithful, even in the face of rejection?

Affirmation:

I choose faithfulness over approval. I will stand firm in my convictions, even when faced with resistance. God's truth is my foundation, and I will not be swayed by the opinions of others. His plans for me are good, and I trust in His divine restoration. I am committed to obedience, knowing that success in His eyes is measured by faithfulness, not popularity.

DAY 32

The Weight of Sin – When Lying Down Means Standing

Welcome to Day 32! You're in the final stretch of this forty-day journey, and today we meet a prophet whose obedience required stillness—literally. Imagine being called by God and instead of running around delivering fiery sermons, He tells you to lie down and not move—for over a year! That's exactly what happened to Ezekiel. For 390 days on one side and 40 days on the other, Ezekiel became a human billboard for Judah's rebellion.

> *"After you have finished this, lie down again, this time on your right side, and bear the sin of the people of Judah. I have assigned you 40 days, a day for each year."*
> ***(Ezekiel 4:6)***

For forty days, Ezekiel's stillness shouted louder than words. His posture wasn't just an endurance test—it was a sermon without speech, an act of obedience that spoke volumes about the weight of sin. Each day represented a year of Judah's sin—a visible, undeniable warning sign to the people. This prophetic act was extreme, uncomfortable, and downright strange, but it wasn't about Ezekiel—it was about calling Judah to repentance.

Speaking of weight, at thirty-two weeks, an expectant mother knows a thing or two about discomfort. With the baby settling into the head-down position, pressure intensifies, shifting everything—lungs feel squished, sleep becomes elusive, and the simplest movements require effort. Just as a mother adjusts to accommodate the growing life within her, Ezekiel had to endure a physical burden to symbolize a spiritual reality. Day after day, Ezekiel laid still, bearing the burden of a nation's rebellion. The discomfort, the patience, the waiting—it all pointed to something greater: Sin carries consequences. Rebellion separates us from God. But even in judgment, God's message was clear—He still desired His people to turn back to Him.

Ezekiel's story reminds us that sin is never just a personal issue—it affects families, communities, and generations. Judah's choices had distanced them from God, and now the consequences were catching up. Yet, even then, God's ultimate goal wasn't destruction—it was restoration. Ezekiel was a living message, a final warning. Would the people listen? Would they turn back? Or would they ignore the signs, assuming they had more time?

Like a mother preparing for labor, knowing that discomfort is temporary but necessary for something greater, Ezekiel's forty-day act challenges us to recognize the weight of sin—not just in our own lives, but in the world around us. Do we grieve over the brokenness we see? Do we pray for those who have drifted away? Or have we become so used to sin that it barely fazes us anymore?

Here's the hard truth: Sin always has a cost. It damages relationships, weakens faith, and distances us from God. Yet, God is always calling us back. He sends warnings, He speaks through His Word, and sometimes He places a burden on our hearts for others. Like Ezekiel, are we willing to stand in the gap—to pray, intercede, and seek God's mercy for those who are lost?

The good news? We don't bear this weight alone. Ezekiel symbolically carried Judah's sins, but Jesus fully carried ours. Because of His sacrifice, we are no longer bound by sin's weight. However, we are still called to acknowledge sin, repent, and walk in righteousness.

Reflection:

- Do I recognize the weight of sin in my life and in the world around me?
- Am I willing to intercede for those who are far from God, just as Ezekiel symbolically did?
- How does knowing that Jesus bore the full burden of sin change the way I live today?

Ezekiel's forty-day assignment was a powerful demonstration of sin's impact, but also of God's relentless call to repentance. Today, we no longer bear sin's weight—Jesus took it upon Himself. But we are still called to pray, intercede, and stand in the gap for others. Will you take up the challenge today?

Affirmation:

I acknowledge the weight of sin, but I refuse to carry what Jesus has already borne for me. I choose to walk in righteousness, interceding for those who are lost and standing in the gap through prayer and obedience. I will not ignore God's warnings but will respond with a heart of repentance and a life devoted to His will. I am an instrument of His mercy, and through me, others will see His grace and truth.

DAY 33

PRIDE POLLUTION – WHEN ARROGANCE CLOUDS THE SOUL

It's Day 33! Ezekiel makes his second appearance on the forty-day podium, but this time, he's not dealing with Israel or Judah—he's confronting Egypt. A lot has happened since his last forty-day stand lying on his side, bearing the sins of Israel and Judah. If you thought that was intense, buckle up—Ezekiel has been on quite a prophetic rollercoaster ever since. From dramatic street performances to stunning visions of God's glory, he's been a living signpost for God's messages. But while his first forty-day prophetic act focused on Israel's downfall, this time, he's been sent to confront the pride of an empire that thought itself untouchable.

Back on Day 23, we tackled pride and jealousy through the life of Saul—a man who let insecurity fester into paranoia, leading to his ultimate downfall. But today, we're dealing with a different kind of pride—not the fragile kind that lashes out in fear, but the towering, arrogant kind that believes it's too great to fall. If Saul was an example of insecure pride, Egypt represents untouchable pride—the kind that ignores every warning and believes its strength is eternal. This is why, even though we already addressed pride, we need to revisit the theme—because arrogance isn't just pride; it's pride that refuses correction.

Unlike Nineveh, which responded to God's warning with repentance, Egypt stood firm in its arrogance—much like a mother experiencing Braxton Hicks contractions and insisting it's the real deal, only to realize it was a false alarm. Egypt mistook its strength for permanence, failing to recognize the warning signs before true labor—the labor of divine judgment—began. And the consequences? A forty-year desolation sentence that would strip the nation of its former glory.

> *"No foot of man shall pass through it, nor foot of beast shall pass through it, and it shall be uninhabited forty years. I will make the land of Egypt desolate among the countries that are desolate, and her cities among the cities that are laid waste shall be desolate forty years; and I will scatter the Egyptians among the nations and disperse them throughout the countries. Yet, thus says the Lord GOD: 'At the end of forty years I will gather the Egyptians from the peoples among whom they were scattered.'"*
> ***(Ezekiel 29:11-13)***

Egypt, the great empire of power and influence, had long trusted in its own strength, wealth, and gods. Pharaohs claimed divine status, and their armies seemed unbeatable. But pride has a way of leading even the strongest to ruin. God's judgment declared that Egypt would be laid waste, its people scattered among the nations, left to experience the kind of helplessness they had never known.

Unlike Nineveh, which repented and was spared, Egypt resisted. Pride can be subtle, but arrogance is loud. It's one thing to struggle with pride in moments of insecurity, but it's another to stand defiantly in self-sufficiency, rejecting every chance to change. Egypt's pride had hardened into arrogance, convincing it that it was too powerful to fall. But God doesn't play by human rules—kingdoms rise and fall at His command, and no empire, no matter how mighty, can stand against His authority.

Yet, even within this judgment, there was a flicker of mercy. After forty years of desolation, God would gather the Egyptians again. They would never reclaim their former dominance, but they would survive. This reminds us that pride leads to downfall, but humility invites restoration.

This prophecy is a mirror for us today. How often do we, like Egypt, trust in our own strength, wisdom, or resources instead of God? Pride convinces us that we are self-sufficient, that we don't need help, and that we can handle life on our own terms—until reality kicks in, much like a growing baby pressing on every organ, reminding the mother that some things are simply beyond her control. But pride is spiritual pollution—it clouds our judgment, poisons relationships, and distances us from God.

Think about it: When was the last time you resisted correction because you "knew better"? Or struggled to ask for help because admitting weakness felt uncomfortable? The lesson from Egypt is clear—the higher we exalt ourselves, the harder the fall. But God always leaves a path for restoration when we choose humility over arrogance.

Reflection:

- Are there areas in my life where I rely more on my own strength than on God?
- How does pride affect my relationship with God and others?
- What does God's promise of restoration teach me about His mercy?

Egypt's forty years of desolation were a direct consequence of its arrogance, but God's mercy provided a way back. The same is true for us—pride may lead to discipline, but humility opens the door to grace. Instead of letting pride pollute our hearts, let's choose to walk in humility, knowing that true strength comes from God alone. What will you surrender today?

Affirmation:

I choose humility over arrogance, knowing that pride leads to downfall, but humility leads to grace. I will not trust in my own strength but will rely fully on God, recognizing that He alone sustains and restores. I surrender my pride, my need for control, and my resistance to correction, allowing God to shape me into His image. My strength is in Him, and my heart is open to His leading.

DAY 34

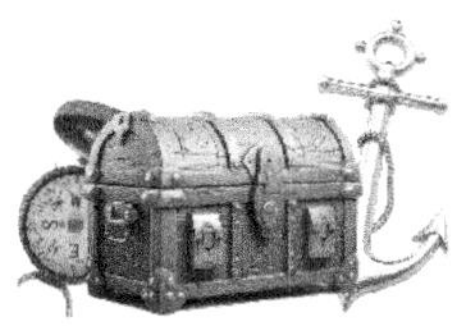

SELFLESSNESS OR SELF-INTEREST?

Welcome to Day 34! I can tell you are anchored! Yesterday, we tackled pride and arrogance, exposing how unchecked self-importance can lead to downfall. Today, let's dig deeper—because if pride is the root, then selfishness, greed, and self-interest are the branches. Pride says, "I'm better than you," but selfishness says, "I come first."

Let's continue our journey of fortification. We've had a fluid appetizer, a patriarchal salad, and palate cleansers along the way. Then God served us a king-sized course, followed by more prophetic refreshment. Now, how about a refreshing beverage to wash it all down? Our next fortified friend has experience serving fancy drinks royally. Though he wasn't a judge, patriarch, prophet, or king, his God-inspired leadership was exceptional after his upgrade from cupbearer.

> *"But the earlier governors—those preceding me—placed a heavy burden on the people and took forty shekels of silver from them in addition to food and wine. Their assistants also lorded it over the people. But out of reverence for God, I did not act like that."*
> ***(Nehemiah 5:15)***

Nehemiah's story is one of resilience and devotion. Though previous governors exploited their authority by taking forty shekels of silver along with food and wine, he chose a different path. Nehemiah saw leadership as a means to serve, not to be served. He set aside personal gain to ensure the well-being of his people, demonstrating selflessness in the face of entitlement. His reverence for God guided his actions, proving that true leadership is marked by sacrifice, not self-indulgence.

By the thirty-fourth week of pregnancy, a mother's focus shifts entirely to the life she is about to bring forth. Her plans revolve around the child's needs, making room for new life even at personal cost. Though sleep is fleeting and comfort is scarce, she willingly bears the weight of the journey, mirroring Nehemiah's selfless devotion to his people. He, too, set aside personal ease to ensure those under his care were not burdened unnecessarily. True fortification is not found in self-preservation but in sacrificial love—the kind that builds, protects, and nurtures without counting the cost.

Each day, we face choices between selflessness and self-interest. In our relationships, workplaces, and daily interactions, we can either give freely or take selfishly. Do we consider the needs of others, or are we only looking out for ourselves? Do we give generously, or do we hold tightly to what we think we deserve?

Nehemiah's example challenges us to examine our hearts. Are we living with a mindset of generosity and care, or are we consumed by personal gain? True fulfillment is not found in how much we take, but in how much we give. Just as Nehemiah fortified the walls of Jerusalem, let us fortify our character—building lives rooted in service, integrity, and selfless love.

Reflection:

- Do I make decisions based on what benefits me or how I can help others?
- In what areas of my life am I holding on too tightly to resources, time, or opportunities rather than using them to bless others?
- How can I practice selflessness today in a way that honors God?

The forty shekels represent the constant choice between self-interest and selflessness. Greed weighs us down, but generosity frees us. Today, choose to give, serve, and love without expecting anything in return. Will you hold on, or will you let go?

Affirmation:

I choose selflessness over self-interest. I will lead with integrity, serve with love, and give without expecting anything in return. My strength comes from God, and my purpose is to bless others. Just as Nehemiah built walls to protect his people, I will build a life rooted in generosity, compassion, and unwavering faith. I am a vessel of God's provision, and through my selflessness, I reflect His love to the world.

DAY 35

THE 40TH BOOK

Welcome to Day 35! Today, we are making a crossover. We are claiming our new character and saying goodbye to the old. We will leave behind self-limiting habits but take the lessons they offered. Now, we enter the New Testament, leaving behind the Old Testament's forty-filled moments and stepping into a new chapter—literally! Faith Fact: Did you know the period between the Old and New Testaments spanned approximately 400 years? That's ten cycles of forty! This time is often referred to as the "silent years" because God was not speaking through prophets. But silent doesn't mean absent—He was still working behind the scenes, orchestrating history to prepare the world for the arrival of the Messiah.

We've examined major forties of the Old Testament, and for the next five days, we'll focus on the New Testament, beginning with the first book of the New Testament—Matthew. So, what does that have to do with the number forty, you ask? Well… Matthew is the 40th book of the Bible, and it's no coincidence that this is the book that introduces Jesus to the world.

> *"The book of the genealogy of Jesus Christ, the son of David, the son of Abraham."*
> ***(Matthew 1:1)***

The Gospel of Matthew is no ordinary book. As the 40th book of the Bible, I need not highlight its significance. And what greater revelation could there be than the introduction of Jesus Christ, the long-awaited Messiah?

For centuries, the people of Israel had waited for the fulfillment of God's promises. Prophets had spoken of a coming King, a Savior who would redeem His people. Then, at last, Matthew opens with the genealogy of Jesus, tracing His lineage from Abraham through David, confirming Him as the fulfillment of every prophecy. The silence between the Old and New Testaments was broken with the arrival of the One who would change history forever.

Much like an expectant mother selecting a name, the Israelites anticipated the identity of their Messiah. A name carries weight—it defines, shapes, and speaks to destiny. Jesus wasn't just any name; it was chosen to signify salvation itself. Just as a mother carefully considers the name of her child, God had already named the Savior of the world, defining His purpose before His birth.

Unlike any other book before it, Matthew introduces Jesus not just as a teacher but as Emmanuel—God with us. Through His words and miracles, Jesus demonstrates the heart of the Father. He calls sinners to repentance, heals the broken, and reveals a kingdom unlike any on earth. The Gospel of Matthew bridges the Old and New Testaments, showing that Jesus is the fulfillment of the law, the promised King, and the hope of the world.

But let's bring this closer to home. The introduction of Jesus in Matthew isn't just historical—it's deeply personal. If Matthew is the book that introduces Jesus, what does your life introduce? When people look at you, do they see Christ reflected? Is your life a book bearing chapters that speak eloquently of the grace, love, kindness, and gentleness of your Savior? Just as Matthew boldly declared Jesus to the world, we, too, are called to reveal Him in our words, actions, and faith.

Matthew signals a transformation, much like the shift from the Old Testament to the New—a transition from waiting to fulfillment, from silence to proclamation. So, what chapter are you stepping into? Will your next season be marked by self-preservation or selfless surrender? The choice is yours, but remember—your life is a gospel in motion. What will it say?

Reflection:

- How has Jesus changed my life, and do I share His story with others?
- If my life were a book, would it introduce Jesus through my character, choices, and faith?
- In what ways can I reflect Christ more clearly to those around me?

Matthew, the 40th book of the Bible, introduces the world to Jesus Christ. But the introduction to Jesus should not end with the Bible—it should continue through us. What story are you telling about Jesus through your life today?

Affirmation:

I am a living testimony of Jesus Christ. My life reflects His love, grace, and truth. I walk in the light of His promises, declaring His goodness in every word, action, and choice. Like Matthew, I introduce Christ to the world through the way I live. My story is a testimony of His transformative power, and I will boldly share His message with those around me.

DAY 36

THE FULFILLMENT OF FORTY

Welcome to Day 36! If you've made it this far, you are officially a member of the Faith-filled Forty Club—forged by faith, tested in trust, and fearfully fortified. You are uncovering God's intriguing patterns, mysteries, and divine blueprints throughout Scripture. So, let's keep digging—because today, we unearth another faith fossil that connects Abraham, Joseph the carpenter, and Jesus in a way that will leave you in awe.

Remember how Matthew carefully outlined the genealogy of Jesus, tracing His lineage all the way back to Abraham? Well, here's something astonishing: from Abraham to Joseph, the earthly father of Jesus, there are 40 generations. Yes—from the father of many nations to the man who would father the Savior of all nations, the number 40 stands tall once again.

> *"As for me, this is my covenant with you: You will be the father of many nations."*
> ***(Genesis 17:4)***

When God made His covenant with Abraham, He launched a promise that would alter the course of history. From Abraham's lineage, a great nation would rise, and ultimately, the Messiah—the Redeemer of the world—would be born. Generations passed, kingdoms rose and fell, but one thing never changed: God never forgot His promise.

And then came Joseph—the 40th name in the lineage of Abraham. Unlike the patriarchs before him, Joseph was not a king, a prophet, or a warrior. He was a humble carpenter—a man whose greatest strength was his faith and obedience. When he discovered that Mary was pregnant, tradition and logic told him to walk away. But Joseph wasn't just any man—he was God's chosen instrument to safeguard and nurture the Son of God. Instead of responding with doubt or fear, he surrendered to the fulfillment of God's promise.

Imagine the weight of that responsibility. Raising Jesus—the Messiah, the fulfillment of centuries of prophecy—yet Joseph did it without fanfare or recognition. He obeyed when the angel told him to take Mary as his wife. He obeyed when God told him to flee to Egypt to protect the child. He obeyed in raising Jesus with love, care, and reverence. Though Joseph's role may have seemed quiet and unremarkable, his faithful obedience ensured that God's redemptive plan stayed on course.

The journey of carrying a promise is never without challenge. Just as an expectant mother patiently endures the unseen work of gestation, waiting for the fullness of time to birth new life, Joseph had to trust the unseen work of God's plan. The weight of responsibility, the uncertainties, the quiet sacrifices—these are the unseen acts of faith that pave the way for divine fulfillment. Like pregnancy, God's promises take time to develop, often requiring patience, endurance, and trust before they manifest in their appointed season.

And isn't that often how God works? He doesn't always call us to spotlight moments—sometimes, He calls us to be faithful in the background, carrying out His will in ways we might never fully comprehend. Just like Joseph, we are often part of a larger, divine masterpiece—one where our obedience has ripple effects beyond what we can see. What promise are you carrying today? Will you trust God's timing, endure the unseen process, and faithfully walk in obedience, knowing that what He has conceived will surely come to pass?

Reflection:

- Have I considered that my obedience today might be fulfilling a promise in someone else's life?

- Do I recognize my role in God's grand plan, even if it seems small?
- When things don't make sense, can I still remain faithful and surrender to God's purpose?

Abraham received the promise. Joseph carried the fulfillment. Where do you stand in God's divine plan? Maybe you are planting the seeds of faith in someone's life. Maybe you are nurturing a promise that is yet to unfold. Or maybe, like Joseph, you are standing in quiet obedience, playing an essential role without even realizing it. No act of faithfulness is wasted. Even when we don't understand everything, we can trust that God is using us in His greater story. Will you remain faithful and surrender to His fulfillment?

Affirmation:

I am a vessel of God's divine plan. My obedience today is part of a greater fulfillment, even when I do not see the full picture. I will trust His timing, embrace my role with humility, and walk in faith, knowing that no act of faithfulness goes unnoticed. I stand firm in His promises, knowing that what He has spoken, He will bring to pass.

DAY 37

The Fulfillment of Forty – Waiting on God's Consolation

You made it to Day 37! Yesterday, we focused on the fathers of promise and the fulfillment from Abraham to Joseph. But today, we arrive at a moment that is not just about waiting—it is about fulfillment. Everything we have studied about the number forty—the flood, the journey to Sinai, the years in the wilderness, the prophetic fasts—all of it has been leading to this. Jesus Christ is the embodiment of transformation, the King of fortification, the One who judges the world and reigns as the King of our lives.

Forty days after His birth, Jesus was presented in the temple, following the custom of purification. What seemed like an ordinary tradition became the moment of fulfilled promise for two faithful servants of God—Simeon and Anna.

> *"Now there was a man in Jerusalem called Simeon, who was righteous and devout. He was waiting for the consolation of Israel, and the Holy Spirit was on him. It had been revealed to him by the Holy Spirit that he would not die before he had seen the Lord's Messiah."*
> ***(Luke 2:25-26)***

Simeon was righteous and devout, a man led by the Holy Spirit. God had given him a promise: he would not die before seeing the Messiah. He waited patiently, year after year, trusting that God would fulfill His word. Then, on this day, prompted by the Spirit, he entered the temple at just the right moment. As he held the infant Jesus in his arms, he knew—this was the Savior, the fulfillment of everything he had been waiting for.

Anna, a prophetess, had also been waiting. She had dedicated her life to prayer and fasting, never leaving the temple. At 84 years old, she had spent decades in worship, anticipating the coming of the Redeemer. When she saw Jesus, she immediately praised God and spoke about Him to all who were looking forward to Israel's redemption.

Their patience, devotion, and connection to the Holy Spirit positioned them to witness the promise fulfilled. Had they grown weary and given up, they might have missed the greatest moment of their lives.

Consider this: a mother waits through forty weeks of gestation before holding her newborn in her arms. Every moment, though hidden from sight, is a divine process of shaping, forming, and preparing. The wait may seem long, even uncomfortable, but when the fullness of time comes, new life emerges. Likewise, God's promises develop within us, unseen yet steadily forming, until the appointed moment of revelation.

Jesus' presentation at the temple was no mere event—it was the declaration that the wait was over. He is the Consolation of Israel, the fulfillment of every prophetic word, the embodiment of every forty that preceded Him. The flood cleansed, Sinai instructed, the wilderness tested, and the fasts prepared—but Jesus completes them all.

This reminds us that God's timing is always perfect. Like Simeon and Anna, we may wait for years, holding on to promises that seem delayed. But if we remain faithful and connected to the Holy Spirit, we will see God's word fulfilled at the appointed time. The fulfillment of forty is here—are you ready to receive Him?

Reflection:

- What promises from God am I waiting for? Am I trusting in His perfect timing?

- Am I actively pursuing a Spirit-led life like Simeon and Anna, or am I distracted by impatience?
- How can I remain faithful in prayer and worship while I wait for God's fulfillment?

Simeon and Anna waited, worshipped, and witnessed. Their patience allowed them to see God's promise come to life. If God has given you a word, trust that it will come to pass in His time. Are you willing to wait faithfully for the fulfillment of His promises?

Affirmation:

I trust in God's perfect timing. I will wait with patience, worship with devotion, and walk in faith, knowing that His promises will be fulfilled. My heart is steadfast, my spirit is aligned with His, and I embrace His divine timing with confidence. Just as Simeon and Anna witnessed the fulfillment of God's word, I too will see His promises come to pass in my life.

DAY 38

Strength in the Wilderness

Welcome to Day 38! We are almost at the end. This statement holds more truth beyond the context of this 40-day journey. Jesus came and purchased our ticket for eternity, giving us the sweetest assurance. And speaking of sweetness, of all the meals served, this is the dessert—we saved the best for last. Unlike earthly sweets, consuming Jesus leaves no guilt, no spike in insulin, no caloric concerns—just pure nourishment for the soul.

Paradoxically, while Jesus is our honey fig and pomegranate ambrosia, what we are about to highlight is the antithesis of indulgence. Throughout His time on earth, Jesus demonstrated how to anchor faith in God. He connected with His Heavenly Father daily, hourly, minutely. Yet, like Elijah and Moses before Him, He undertook the ultimate journey for transformation—a forty-day expedition in the wilderness with no lunchbox or water bottle. His sustenance? Spirit-soufflé.

> *"After fasting forty days and forty nights, he was hungry."*
> ***(Matthew 4:2)***

Before Jesus began His public ministry, He was led by the Spirit into the wilderness—a place of solitude, testing, and preparation. For forty days and forty nights, He fasted and prayed, drawing strength not from food, but from communion with the Father.

This was no ordinary fast. It was a battle of the spirit. After His time of fasting, Satan came, offering Jesus shortcuts to power, provision, and glory. Turn these stones to bread. Throw yourself down and let the angels catch you. Bow down, and I'll give you the world. Each temptation sought to pull Jesus away from His divine mission.

But Jesus, though physically weak, was spiritually fortified. He responded not with human reasoning, but with the Word of God. He did not give in to the desires of the flesh, nor did He waver in His identity. His time in the wilderness was not just about denying the body, but about empowering the spirit.

Much like a child in the womb anticipating delivery, the body craves relief, yet the moment must be divinely appointed. The waiting, though challenging, is purposeful—strengthening, refining, preparing for the fullness of what is to come. A mother, eager to push, must also trust in the perfect timing of birth. Likewise, Jesus' wilderness journey was not just about endurance but about perfect alignment—waiting on the Father's timing to step into His calling.

This challenges us: How do we respond in our wilderness seasons? Like Jesus, you will endure severe testing, but take heart—He conquered and won the victory, and so can we. When faced with trials, temptations, and spiritual battles, do we feed the flesh or strengthen the spirit? Jesus showed us that fasting and prayer are powerful tools for overcoming temptation and aligning with God's will. When we deny ourselves, we make room for more of God. When we set aside distractions, we hear His voice more clearly.

Forty days of fasting prepared Jesus for His calling—what might God be preparing you for?

Reflection:

- How do I handle times of spiritual testing—do I draw closer to God or look for quick solutions?
- Have I ever experienced the power of fasting and prayer? How can I incorporate these into my spiritual life?

- What temptations do I face that I need to combat with the Word of God?

Jesus' forty days in the wilderness were not a time of weakness, but of spiritual strengthening. Fasting and prayer realign us with God's will and prepare us for greater purpose. If God is leading you into a season of spiritual discipline, will you embrace it or seek an easy way out? What are you willing to surrender to be strengthened?

Affirmation:

I am strengthened through the trials I face. I will not seek shortcuts, but will trust in God's perfect plan for my life. Through fasting, prayer, and obedience, I align myself with His will. Like Jesus, I stand firm on the Word of God, knowing that in my weakness, His strength is made perfect. My spirit is fortified, my purpose is clear, and I walk boldly in victory.

DAY 39

FORTIFIED THROUGH LASHES

Welcome to Day 39! Can you feel it? That electric anticipation, like the final moments before a long-awaited birth? We've traveled through valleys of testing, climbed mountains of revelation, and now, we stand on the precipice of fulfillment. The labor pains of this journey are intensifying, and the delivery is near. Just as an expectant mother feels the pressing urgency to push, we too must brace ourselves—because today, we face the refining fire of endurance.

This journey has never been about ease. No, fortification is forged through fire. Like Jesus, like Paul, like Stephen, we will endure severe testing. But take heart—He conquered and won the victory, and so can we.

Stephen stood before the Sanhedrin, falsely accused, knowing that his life was hanging in the balance. Yet, when given the opportunity to speak, he did not beg for mercy. He did not defend himself with human arguments or attempt to escape his fate. Instead, he testified.

> *"After forty years had passed, an angel appeared to Moses in the flames of a burning bush in the desert near Mount Sinai... He led them out of Egypt and performed wonders and signs in Egypt, at the Red Sea, and for forty years in the wilderness."*
> ***(Acts 7:30, 36)***

His words were not his own; they were Scripture. In his final moments, he delivered a sweeping summary of Israel's history—a treasure chest brimming with the trials and triumphs of forty. He spoke of Moses, who spent forty years in Egypt, forty years in the wilderness, and another forty years leading the Israelites. He recalled the forty years Israel wandered, tested and refined by God. Every mention of "forty" was a reminder: God uses time to prepare His people, to shape their faith, and to reveal His purpose.

Stephen's speech was not just a history lesson—it was a revelation. He pointed to Jesus as the fulfillment of everything that had come before. Just as Israel had rejected Moses, the people had now rejected Christ. Just as the Israelites had resisted God's leading in the wilderness, they had resisted the Messiah sent to redeem them. Stephen saw the pattern, and he called it out boldly, refusing to shrink in fear, even as the crowd turned against him.

Then, as the stones were lifted, Stephen looked up. He did not see doom or despair. He saw Jesus—standing at the right hand of God. Not seated, as Scripture often describes Him, but standing—watching, approving, welcoming. The One whom Stephen had testified about was now testifying for him.

Similarly, Paul, a servant of Christ, bore the lashes himself. In 2 Corinthians 11:24, he recounts, "Five times I received from the Jews the forty lashes minus one." The Jews, careful not to exceed the prescribed punishment, stopped at thirty-nine. Yet, even in their restraint, Paul was beaten and bruised, suffering for the gospel. He endured not because he was guilty, but because he was faithful.

And then, there was Jesus—the innocent Lamb, whipped beyond measure. Roman soldiers did not count His lashes. They did not stop at thirty-nine. They stripped Him, mocked Him, and tore His flesh without restraint. Each lash was undeserved, yet each was taken out of love. The One who knew no sin took the full weight of our punishment.

The law of forty lashes was meant to correct the guilty. But Jesus, the innocent Son of God, bore lashes of love—for you, for me, for the world.

Reflection:

- If I were falsely accused like Stephen, would I still stand firm in my faith?
- How well do I know the story of Scripture? Could I testify of God's work in history and in my own life?
- Paul endured lashes for the gospel—what am I willing to endure for my faith?
- When I discipline or correct others, do I do so with justice and mercy, or with harshness?
- Am I living as someone truly redeemed by Christ's suffering, or do I take His sacrifice for granted?

As Christians, we will be persecuted for righteousness. We will be mocked, ridiculed, and despised. Our convictions will be questioned, our faith tested, and our commitment challenged. The world may try to silence us, to make us cower in fear. But we must remember—Christ bore the lashes first. He endured the ultimate rejection so that we might stand in the victory of His resurrection. If He, the perfect Son of God, was willing to suffer for us, how much more should we be willing to suffer for His name?

Will we shrink in the face of opposition, or will we stand firm, fortified in faith? Will we endure for the sake of righteousness, or will we bow to the pressures of the world? Now is the time to decide.

Affirmation:

I am fortified through faith, strengthened by trials, and victorious in Christ. No opposition can shake my foundation, for I stand firm in His truth. I will not cower in fear but will proclaim His name boldly. Just as Jesus bore the lashes of love for me, I will endure for His sake. My faith is unshakable, my purpose is clear, and I am victorious in Him.

DAY 40

FORTIFIED FOR FLIGHT

You made it to Day 40! Congratulations! You should be feeling fresh, fine, and fired up. Today, you should be both full and empty—full of joy, wisdom, and divine revelation, yet empty of anything that held you back. You should be hungry, famished, and craving more of God, yet completely satisfied in Him. Like Noah, Isaac, Moses, Othniel, Deborah, Gideon, David, Solomon, Jeremiah, Ezekiel, Jonah, Paul, Stephen, and Jesus—all who have had their "forty-fied" encounters—you, too, stand at the threshold of transformation.

> *"After His suffering, He presented Himself to them and gave many convincing proofs that He was alive. He appeared to them over a period of forty days and spoke about the kingdom of God."*
> ***(Acts 1:3)***

For forty days after His resurrection, Jesus walked the earth, revealing Himself to His followers. He had conquered death, yet He did not immediately ascend. Instead, He remained, appearing to many, proving beyond all doubt that He was alive. His presence was not fleeting—it was a declaration of victory, a confirmation of His power, and an invitation into something greater.

Imagine the disciples—confused, heartbroken, their faith hanging by a thread. They had seen Him die. They had watched as His lifeless body was placed in a tomb, and with it, their hopes seemingly buried forever. But then—He appeared. The same Jesus who had been crucified now stood before them, speaking, eating, and teaching. His resurrecting power was undeniable. It was personal. It was transformative.

Each of those forty days carried a profound message. To Mary Magdalene, He turned mourning into joy. To the disciples on the road to Emmaus, He unveiled hidden truths. To Thomas, He replaced doubt with unshakable faith. Every encounter was intentional, every moment was preparation.

But Jesus did not stay just to comfort them—He stayed to commission them. The Great Commission was not given in theory—it was birthed in those forty days. He reminded them of the kingdom of God, empowered them with His Spirit, and sent them forth with the greatest mission ever given: to make disciples of all nations.

And now, the question lingers—what will you do with your forty days? What has been conceived in you during this journey? Because just as a mother, having endured the waiting, the stretching, and the labor, reaches the moment of delivery, you, too, are at the moment of birthing something new. The contractions of faith, the growing pains of obedience, the stirring deep within your spirit has all been leading to this.

Jesus is still revealing Himself. He is still calling. He is still commissioning. But He is also coming again! After appearing for forty days, He ascended to heaven, promising to return for us. The real question is—are we ready to return with Him? Are we prepared to board the first-class flight to Paradise, the most luxurious destination beyond the highest-rated resorts of this world? Heaven awaits, and the best and longest vacation of all time has already been booked and paid for by the Lamb. Will you be ready to board?

This is not the end—it is only the beginning. You have been fortified. Now, it is time to take flight.

Reflection:

- How have I experienced the resurrecting power of Jesus in my own life?
- Do I live as though Jesus is truly alive, or do I still struggle with doubt and fear?

- Jesus revealed Himself to prepare His followers for a mission—how am I sharing His power with others?

Affirmation:

I am fortified in Christ and prepared to take flight. I will walk in the power of His resurrection, unshaken by fear, unwavering in faith, and unrelenting in my mission. My life will reflect His victory, and I will proclaim His truth boldly. I am chosen, empowered, and ready to soar into the divine purpose He has ordained for me.

Meet the Author

Hilette Virgo is a passionate Christian Life Coach, faith-based author, publisher, and transformational speaker dedicated to helping individuals deepen their walk with God. As the CEO of Great-Nest Publishing Inc. and Great-Nest Coaching Academy, she empowers aspiring authors and spiritual seekers to unlock their God-given potential through writing, mentorship, and personal development.

With an insatiable passion for biblical mysteries and divine patterns, Hilette is committed to uncovering the profound significance of numbers in Scripture. Her latest work, *40 Days to a Fortified Life*, is designed to guide readers into a spiritually fortified experience. To complement the book, she has also created the 40 Days to a Fortified Life Coaching Guide and Fortification Journal, providing additional tools for those seeking a structured and transformational journey.

Beyond writing, Hilette serves as a mentor and coach, equipping individuals to embrace their divine purpose. She specializes in ghostwriting, editing, book coaching, and publishing services, assisting aspiring authors in bringing their God-inspired messages to life.

She is also the Founder of Purple Pearls Ministries, a faith-based platform that empowers women through the written and spoken word and transformative events. Through this ministry, she helps women embrace their divine calling and walk confidently in their God-given identity.

Other Works by Hilette Virgo

- *Activating Her Eagle Instincts*
- *Evoking Your Divine Dove*
- *Do the Write Thing Today!*
- *Visionary for the Waiting in the Pit (3-part series)*

Upcoming Releases

📖 *I AM—My Knight in Shining Armor*

📖 *Meaningful Mentorship: A Spiritual Mentor's Handbook*

📖 *Other Books in the Sacred Numbers: Unlocking God's Divine Code in Scripture Series*

📖 *Purple Pearls Anthology Series*

For coaching inquiries, speaking engagements, ghostwriting, editing, book coaching, or publishing services, contact Hilette at:

📩 **hilettevirgomotivates@gmail.com**

📩 **greatnestpublications@gmail.com**

Connect with Hilette Virgo

- **Facebook:** @HiletteVirgoMotivates
- **Instagram:** @HiletteVirgo
- **YouTube:** *Hilette Virgo Motivates*

Made in the USA
Columbia, SC
23 February 2025

54284933R00109